I0825187

Praise for

The Well-Educated Child

"Deborah Kenny sounds a clarion call. Read this book and see how, with steely clarity and unwavering moral conviction, even the boldest educational aims can be achieved."

—Sam Wineburg, Margaret Jacks Chair of Education, Emeritus, Stanford University

"This moving and insightful book is truly a gift."

—Pedro A. Noguera, PhD, dean of Rossier School of Education, University of Southern California

"A remarkable, compelling story. This book is both inspirational and practical."

—Ron Berger, former chief academic officer at EL Education

"A must-read for anyone who cares about American public education."

—Deborah Meier, founder of Central Park East Elementary School and author of *The Power of Their Ideas*

"*The Well-Educated Child* is destined to become a classic."

—Ed Lewis, founder of *Essence* magazine

"Utterly absorbing. *The Well-Educated Child* is essential reading for parents and educators."

—Howard Fuller, distinguished professor emeritus at Marquette University, former superintendent of Milwaukee Public Schools, and founder of Black Alliance for Educational Options

"Part memoir, part roadmap, in *The Well-Educated Child*, Deborah Kenny shares knowledge and insights that could change the way we educate students for the future."

—Zaretta Hammond, MA, teacher, educator, and author of *Culturally Responsive Teaching and the Brain* and *Rebuilding Students' Learning Power*

"I'm deeply moved by Deborah Kenny's vision for what schools can and should be. A personal, practical, and compelling guide for anyone who wants to help children reach their full potential."

—Sheryl Sandberg, founder and author of *Lean In*

"This beautifully crafted, engaging book would make a great book club choice for teachers, administrators, and parents."

—Shelley Harwayne, founder of the Manhattan New School and former superintendent of NYC District 2

"Deborah Kenny is a once in a generation visionary. She believes that our children deserve the highest quality education and works to ensure they receive it."

—Melba Wilson, founder of Melba's Restaurant

The Well-Educated Child

---

by

DEBORAH KENNY

Foreword by JOHN LEGEND

GET LIFTED BOOKS
A zando IMPRINT
NEW YORK

Get Lifted Books is an imprint of Zando.
zandoprojects.com

First Edition: April 2026

Text design by Neuwirth & Associates, Inc.
Cover design by Christopher Brian King

Library of Congress Control Number: 2025947337

978-1-63893-332-8 (hardcover)
978-1-63893-364-9 (ebook)

10 9 8 7 6 5 4 3 2 1
Manufactured in the United States of America
LKS

For Tyler Joel

CONTENTS

Foreword

BY JOHN LEGEND

This summer, our house has been a revolving door of kids racing between camps—cooking camp, basketball camp, fashion and design camp. Some days they come home covered in glitter. Other days, it's bruises and grass stains. If I'm being honest, part of the reason we sign them up is pure survival. Four kids under ten with nothing to do all day? They will turn the house into a full-blown wrestling ring.

But mostly, it's about discovery. Letting my kids try things and letting them fail. Camp gives our kids space to explore, to test out their voices, their confidence, their curiosity, when no one is telling them who to be. It helps them figure out how to be in different rooms, with different people and different challenges, and still feel like themselves.

Isn't that what we all want for our kids? Not perfection but preparation. That as they grow, they feel deeply loved, sure of themselves, and confident in who they are. That they're prepared not just to do well in school, but to shape the world that will exist long after we're gone.

That's why I deeply believe in what Deborah Kenny has built with Harlem Village Academies.

My first trip to HVA was in 2010. The hallways were quiet, but it wasn't the quiet of control. It was a purposeful quiet. The kind that comes when everyone knows why they are there. The students were confident, and the teachers were respectful. I could feel the love in the air: strong and structured. The kind of love that says, I see you. I expect greatness from you. I'll walk with you to get there.

Deborah and I had lunch after, and I remember thinking, *This woman is electric*. The way she spoke about education wasn't abstract or polite. It was personal. Urgent. She wasn't trying to build a "good school for Harlem." She was building a school that would rival the best in the country, a school that could compete with the Sidwell Friends and Scarsdales of the world. Deborah didn't just reject the idea that urban schools should be judged by a lower standard. She was offended by it.

Too often the education system in this country sends an unspoken message: Some children are meant to govern, and others are meant to be governed. Some are encouraged to question, analyze, and lead. Others are expected to sit still, memorize, and repeat. Curiosity gets treated like a luxury. Like critical thinking belongs only to certain kids, from certain neighborhoods. Like rigor, beauty, and joy are reserved for someone else's children.

Deborah has built something radically different with HVA.

Her schools teach young people to read deeply, to think critically, and to speak boldly. The goal isn't just high test scores (though they have those). It's not just getting kids into college (though they do that too). It's about nurturing minds that are nimble and ready to engage with a world that is fast-changing and complex. Ready to spot truth from misinformation. Ready to challenge ideas. Prepared to become citizens, not just of their neighborhoods, but of the world.

I've stayed connected to HVA for more than a decade. I have performed with students, and I wrote their school song, "We Rise." One of the most moving moments of my career was watching those students sing it back to me—every lyric and note was full of pride. What they were singing wasn't just a performance. It was a declaration.

The Well-Educated Child is an invitation into that world.

This is not just a theory—it's a story deeply lived. Deborah begins with a teacher who opened her heart to learning and goes on to share what it means to build a school grounded in love and high expectations. She reminds us that joy and academic rigor are not opposites. That great teaching means helping children learn how to think, not just how to follow. And that the foundation of a great school is not only a strong curriculum but a culture that sees children not as problems to fix but as people to honor.

She also calls out what so many tiptoe around: that our current system often works exactly as designed. That unless we fight for something different, unless we demand that our schools reflect the brilliance and potential of every child, we will keep recreating the same inequities over and over again.

As a father of four, I read this book through two lenses. The first one is public: I've supported HVA for more than a decade, and I believe it's a model worth spreading. The second lens is personal: I want my kids to live in a world where their minds are nourished and their questions are welcomed. I want them to learn how to build community. And how to care for others.

That is the spirit of HVA. And this book doesn't just tell the story; it shows us how to do the work.

Whether you're guiding a child, standing at the front of a classroom, or simply passionate about learning, this book has something for you. There is something in these pages for all of us who want to dream bigger for our kids and do better by them.

Enjoy this book. Share it. Let it challenge you. Let it inspire you. Let it remind you: Our children rise when we rise to meet them.

The Well-Educated Child

Introduction

We send our children to school hoping that they will become insightful, knowledgeable, principled, independent. Hoping, essentially, that they will become well educated.

But the reality is that American public education is deeply deficient. Cognitive rigor is scarce; student engagement is low. A Gates Foundation study found that the teaching of complex thinking was absent in 80 percent of middle school classrooms.[1] Researchers at Yale reported that 69 percent of high school students say that they are bored in school.[2] In 2024, the National Assessment of Educational Progress (known as "the Nation's Report Card") found US academic performance "devastating," with only 30 percent of eighth graders proficient in reading, only 28 percent in math. The latter result places the US thirty-fourth out of the thirty-eight advanced industrial nations.[3]

Clearly the prevailing approach in our nation's schools is wholly inadequate.

This book sets forth my vision of an ideal K–12 education: the attributes and skills that children should have by the time they graduate from high school and the principles and practices by which schools can instill them. It also offers ideas that parents can use to contribute to their children's education.

My perspective comes from a lifetime in education, including many years as a teacher and camp counselor, my considered approach to parenting, the exquisite teaching I've observed in private schools, and over two decades running PreK–12 schools. I've spent thousands of hours in classrooms studying the finer points of pedagogy.

I start with a simple but fundamental question: What does it mean to be well educated? In my view, students who are well educated can reason independently, understand ideas deeply, and evaluate information critically. They are self-directed and self-motivated. Students who are well educated are too astute to be duped by misinformation; they are independent minded but not irrational, confident but not arrogant, spirited but civil in discourse. They are kind, happy, and considerate of others, not self-centered and stressed. They have cultivated an appreciation for beauty: the beauty of art, of music, the beauty of math. They are knowledgeable and well-read but have the humility to know how much they don't know. All this is what I wanted for my own children. It is what I believe all children deserve.

For a school to produce well-educated students, it needs to offer instruction that is cognitively demanding, with intriguing questions that spark intellectual curiosity and cultivate intrinsic motivation. A curriculum that immerses students in the world's great books, ideas, and thinkers. Assessments that require students to demonstrate their ability to apply knowledge and skills in unfamiliar contexts. A school culture that teaches self-management and instills an abiding moral compass and a sense of purpose.

I founded Harlem Village Academies in 2003 with this vision in mind. Every year for ten years, we welcomed a new group of fifth graders with bright eyes and hopeful smiles. But their previous schools were dangerous and chaotic and had failed them. As a result, they entered years behind, and it took an immense amount of time just to catch them up to grade level. We worked around the clock with all our hearts. We created a calm, warm, orderly environment, meticulously refining every aspect of our schools, and instilled a passion for reading and learning. By 2007, our schools ranked number one in math in New York State and outperformed the city and state across all subjects. Since then, HVA has consistently been considered among the highest performing group of schools in the country.

But when schools are ranked "number one" or called "high performing," it usually only means that students excel on state tests. I wanted so much more for our children. I wanted them to become well educated in the way I described above, that is, to experience what educators now call deeper learning: pedagogy that develops the high-level thinking and masterful work that are expected at the best private schools. So in 2012, I assembled a brain trust of some of the leading educational thinkers of our time, the master teachers of the master teachers. We studied and worked intensively: drafting principles, piloting practices in the classroom, reflecting on setbacks, trying again. I made plenty of mistakes along the way. But it was often the mistakes that led to the most profound insights, to a clarity and depth of understanding about what comprises a world-class education.

And that is why I was compelled to write this book. I felt a responsibility to share what I have learned—all that I wish I had known when I first started out as a teacher and parent—so that the next generation of educators does not have to struggle as much as we did, and so parents can know how to guide their children at home, what to look for in a school, and how to partner with their schools. Part I chronicles our origin story and start-up years through our work with those brilliant master educators. Part II describes what it means to be well educated, and why a foundation of free inquiry, humility, passion for knowledge, and appreciation for beauty is vital for students. It then takes up assessment: how it can support or hinder student learning. Part III details the three core elements of an exceptional education—quality thinking, agency, and ethical purpose—and examines why they matter for children.

The ultimate purpose of this book is to alter the trajectory of American public schooling and to help teachers and parents ensure that the children in their care receive a truly excellent education. The task is urgent, as the quality of our children's education largely determines the nature of society.

It has been my great good fortune to learn from the most brilliant minds in the field, among them Debbie Meier, one of the most influential educators of the last half century, who has done the actual hard work of teaching in and leading schools. In discussing with Debbie the idea of writing this book, I confided that I was hesitant. While I felt a responsibility to share what we had learned, I said, there was still so much to do to fully actualize my vision. Debbie insisted that the right time is now. "You aim for the ideal, but you never actually get there. You just keep working at it," she said. "These are important ideas. People are looking to do what you've done. Invite them to join you."[4]

This book, then, is an invitation. The principles and practices elucidated in these pages can guide us to a new era in public education. I invite you to learn with me as we aspire to make our nation's schools worthy of our children.

Let's get to work.

Part I

1.

Something Greater than Oneself

One August afternoon when I was nineteen, a friend and I were driving back to New York City from our summer camp upstate. Somewhere along the way, we saw a sign with a single word and an arrow pointing right. The word was *Utopia*.

"Take a right!" I blurted out. "We have to check—just in case!" As he drove up the dirt road, we broke up laughing.

Of course, our roadside utopia turned out to be a dive bar.

I have always been intrigued by utopia. In college that spring, I had taken a course called The Utopian Imagination. While I had learned that "utopias are intrinsically unattainable,"[1] I didn't really accept the idea. I felt unmoored when people spoke about being "realistic," which seemed to be code for settling. This conviction may have been innate, but mainly it came from experience. I believed in utopia because I believed that I'd already experienced it.

It was at that camp, where I had spent summers since ninth grade.

Like many students, I felt bored and disconnected in high school. But camp was another world. Camp was where I got my real education. For four years as a camper then three as a counselor, I was surrounded by serious thinkers, educators, and activists.

Our counselors had come of age in the sixties. They were witty, well-read, confident. They were burning idealists with an insatiable intellectual curiosity. And they believed that we should "replace power rooted in possession, privilege, or circumstance by power and uniqueness rooted in love, reflectiveness, reason, and creativity," as Students for a Democratic Society had written in 1962.[2] They read James Baldwin, Betty Friedan, D. H. Lawrence, Kafka, Ginsberg, and Jack Kerouac—who could have been speaking about them when he wrote that "the only people for me are the mad ones, the ones who are mad to live, mad to talk . . . who never say a commonplace thing."[3] I admired them intensely.

Most of all, I admired Mel, the camp's iconic senior counselor and master teacher. Born in the Bronx in 1928 to Russian immigrants, Mel had been the camp's unofficial lead educator for decades. It was a Jewish camp with kids from all over the country, and hundreds of teenagers would sit cross-legged on the floor for hours, mesmerized as Mel elucidated the Jewish ethical code of responsibility for the vulnerable and disenfranchised. While not conventionally religious, Mel would cite religious precepts related to social justice: "one law for the stranger and the citizen," "justice, justice, shalt thou pursue," "do not hold back the wages of the worker overnight." His lectures were riveting, seductive, substantive; you could hear a pin drop. He treated us like serious young adults capable of thinking seriously about the world.

Under his guidance and that of the counselors he mentored, we argued endlessly about ideas. Sitting on the ground in circles under apple trees in the large grass field, we learned about history, ethics, literature, politics, philosophy. The arguments that started in those circles often extended into dinner and sometimes further into the evening. There was a lot of Emerson, Baldwin, *I and Thou*, *Siddhartha*, Dylan Thomas. One day, we were told to study an issue, select which side of the debate we agreed with, then prepare to argue the other side. While I didn't fully realize it at the time, this philosophical interrogation of one another's opinions, this ongoing reasoning and discourse, came directly from the Jewish tradition of arguing with good intentions to sharpen one's mind and arrive at the best conclusion. The ethos was to be knowledgeable but skeptical, to be nonconformist, to question authority. But it wasn't simply rebellion. We were expected to defend our thinking.

The atmosphere was warm and welcoming, friendly and loving; there were all kinds of kids but no cliques, so everyone felt like they belonged. We were taught to be accepting and kind to one another. We were taught to think of ourselves as—to use one of our favorite words—a community. That is why we sat in circles all the time. That is why we sang together. During free periods, we often found ourselves going for long walks together, talking for hours about our innermost feelings. The intellectual camaraderie, the emotional intimacy—it all made us feel a deep kinship with one another. The close friendships I made have lasted all of my life.

Each aspect of the camp program had an educational purpose. Learning was challenging and interesting. Texts and topics were intentionally nuanced, which taught us to be discerning and skeptical. We were often asked about what we believed or cared about or might do if we faced difficult choices, all of which developed self-awareness, the foundation of agency. Overnight hiking trips had us pushing through exhaustion and fear (we were once given the choice of two hikes, one of which required jumping off a tall cliff into water), which instilled self-reliance and persistence. Our mantra was "peer leadership," meaning that we were expected to take the lead in discussions and activities, while the adults (who were called "advisors") guided us to do that well. This cultivated confidence and self-direction. Through all these experiences, we began to think deeply about our lives.

Mel was a Hebrew school principal in New Jersey, and those of us who grew up there got to see him during the school year as well. He was a relentless talent scout, personally recruiting the very best educators from the camp staff to teach at his school, and vice versa. His style was irreverent. He would flout authority, break rules ("You can study on the bus. This is more important than a fucking math test!"), start singing at the drop of a hat, and tell fictitious stories just to see how long it took us to catch on. But he could be intensely serious. When one of his teachers (my first camp counselor) approached him for guidance about a humanitarian crisis in Ethiopia, Mel galvanized his students to write op-eds, organize, and light a fire under their friends. Soon, busloads of teenagers were pouring into United Nations Plaza for a rally that garnered national media attention, with Mel standing in the background so the students could shine. He had done this his entire life, like back in 1963 when he drove students to the March on Washington. He took the same approach when engaging us in activism: encouraging us to take the lead. We rallied in solidarity with farm laborers, raised funds to alleviate child famine, organized visits to sing in nursing homes, and protested the imprisonment of Soviet political dissidents when the Bolshoi Ballet came to Lincoln Center.

In camp, too, we looked for ways to live by our ideals. We took turns serving and cleaning up in the dining hall. The oldest kids lived in tents in a miniature commune in the woods, growing vegetables, tending chickens (and a cow!), setting up a daily work schedule, and taking responsibility, through collective decision-making, for governing the community. "We didn't ask who was in charge," one kid said. "*We* were in charge."

My favorite part of the day was after dinner: communal singing. First, we'd learn the meaning of the Hebrew lyrics. One song, for example, was based on a Talmudic passage about "the work," which means the work of repairing the world:

You are not obligated to complete the work,
But neither are you at liberty to neglect it.

Singing together drew us close to each other and to our inner selves. For me, music was a spiritual experience. Sometimes I would close my eyes and it felt like I was floating.

And the nights—the nights were something else. We'd sit around a campfire, some kids playing guitar, some with their arms around each other, all of us singing. Bob Dylan. Neil Young. Our own little Woodstock, a decade after Woodstock. Under the stars, euphoric.

On the last day of camp, we'd stay up all night, walking around the fields in a kind of daze, holding on to the final hours, talking until sunrise. "We lived a charmed life this summer," a friend said one year.

And then, a caravan of buses would show up to bring us back to reality.

When I got back home to the suburbs, the cognitive dissonance was deafening. I felt disconnected from "normal" life. Things that made sense to everyone else did not make sense to me. Things that were important to others felt ephemeral or boring to me. What seemed radical to them seemed normal to me. At camp—with its focus on big ideas and important thinkers—we had studied the lives of people who changed the world and we had talked about how we could change the world ourselves. I came to see American society—with its focus on materialism, status, and upward mobility—as supremely superficial. I did not understand why everyone just went along with it. Success was unappealing. Intellectual struggle was appealing.

In eleventh grade, an English teacher asked me to become the editor of the school paper. "It will look good on your college resume," a guidance counselor said. That and similar experiences got me wondering: Am I supposed to do well in high school just to get into a good college just to get a good job just to work my way up to a better job just to—what? In twenty years, I'll be exactly where I am now, asking what it was for. This line of reasoning drew me further into questions about the meaning of life in general and the purpose of my life in particular.

In college, these questions became the main thing that interested me. The inner life came to be the only thing that felt real. Freshman year, I must have read Rilke's *Letters to a Young Poet* a hundred times. It was like he and I were meeting each night to talk. "Nobody can counsel and help you. No one," Rilke said. "There is only one single way. Search . . ."

I took up this search full-time—in courses on intellectual history, philosophy, literature, and religion; in long conversations with fellow students; in the library reading Aldous Huxley, William James, Allen Ginsberg, Emerson, Thoreau. And at off-campus lectures, like one by Ram Dass, who spoke about transcending limitations. "Somewhere along the line you realize you aren't who you thought you were," he said. I was drawn to professors, rabbis, artists—anyone who might have the inside track on the nature of Truth. I remember overhearing a dorm counselor say to my roommate, "Debbie could be in a room with a hundred people and she would still be alone."

Meanwhile, each summer, I would return to camp as a counselor. I asked Mel to place me in his group so I could learn from him directly. I observed his technique, his pacing and cadence, the way he would whisper softly to draw you in. I absorbed the way he maintained a visceral connection with the group as a whole while also remaining attentive to each student individually. He taught us to captivate students at the very start of a lesson and to make sure that the ending was strong ("Cut it at the peak!" he'd say). He taught us that a close emotional bond between teacher and student was foundational. His kids cared about learning because they felt how much he loved them and how passionate he was about his subject matter. Above all, Mel and the other senior counselors taught us that the most important way to influence students is by personal example. That was the creed: personal example.

For grad school, I applied to Columbia to study education. I loved every minute of those classes. Our first assignment was to write an essay on our educational philosophy. "Do not seek out a neat package of convenient and efficient formulas to mechanically repeat," I wrote. "Teach what you love." I thought perhaps after teaching I might become a school principal, but a professor talked me out of it. "You wouldn't have the patience for the city bureaucracy," she said.

Decades later, after Mel had retired, I would call him periodically. One time, I asked him how he'd learned to be a teacher. Sharp as ever, he replied, "You're asking me that now, when I'm fucking ninety-two years old?" Typical Mel. Even over the phone, I could see the sparkle in his eyes. "Okay, seriously," he went on, "I learned by experience. That, and constantly reading. And I learned from the principal where I started. He was an amazing teacher."

"*You* were an amazing teacher," I said.

"My little Debbie, I love you."

"I love you too, Mel."

He had known me since I was twelve years old.

One afternoon a few months later, I was finishing a principals meeting when a dozen texts from friends came in at once: "Did you hear?" "Call me . . ." "Are you okay?"

Mel had died. Mel, our teacher whom we loved.

"No," I texted back. I was not okay. I was heartbroken.

In the days that followed, we all shared stories and tributes. One former counselor wrote: "I well remember our revolutionary intense discussions and experiences together. Bowing my head in gratitude that I was gifted to be a part of the miracle that was those years."

In the evenings, we would seek each other out, lifelong friends reminiscing for hours. "He told me *I* was his favorite," we said, laughing through tears. Some of us said the Mourner's Kaddish (a prayer recited after the death of a loved one) together over FaceTime.

I had been asked to speak about Mel before: at camp to dedicate a building in his honor; in the East Village at a lifetime award ceremony. And now, one final time, at a memorial service for our Mel. Hundreds of camp alumni from around the world gathered on Zoom, and I asked my three children to join, as I longed for them to know him. Addressing the community, my heart heavy, I said, "Mel imbued our lives with hope because he taught us everything that we needed to know to do something about the injustices in the world. So, losing him, beyond a personal loss, might feel like the loss of that hope. But it's fitting that we are gathered to speak about Mel on MLK weekend. Mel had marched with Dr. King, who famously said, 'Injustice anywhere is a threat to justice everywhere,' and Mel taught us how to take that idea and turn it into the way we live our lives."

We all knew that we had been fortunate to have had him as our teacher and to have received this exceptional education. We had experienced what it is to understand ideas deeply, to think independently, to be a community, and to be part of something greater than oneself. Once you have gotten an education like this, you are never the same.

When I founded Harlem Village Academies, I envisioned this kind of exceptional education for the children we would serve. Schools could be utopian communities where students were challenged intellectually, nurtured emotionally, and enriched spiritually. Schools could be places where brilliant, idealistic educators fulfilled their calling while building the groundwork for—and striving to create a microcosm of—a transcendent society. Back then, I believed all this was possible.

I still do.

2.

All Evidence to the Contrary Notwithstanding

During my last summer at camp, Mel's wife had asked me if I was interested in any of the boys that I was spending time with. I told her no, I hadn't met the perfect person yet. "There's no such thing as a perfect person," she replied. A few years later, I told her that it turned out there was.

His name was Joel. He was a graduate student in philosophy and religion, liked football, loved Hendrix, painted, played guitar. He took my breath away. It was the kind of love that you would give your life for. We married at twenty-five.

Joel was kind, soft spoken, well-read, intellectually curious—and hilarious. He talked to our three kids the same way he did to adults, with a dry wit that made me laugh all the time. He taught them how to identify trees on nature walks, draw a daffodil, plant a garden, build a custom model rocket launcher. Whatever they asked, he would drop what he was doing and focus on them.

One day, out of the blue, Joel said that he felt dizzy. Two

days later, before we knew what was happening, he was diagnosed with leukemia. We were shattered. But we each kept up a positive spirit for the other. Only Joel could write a list of "The Pros and Cons of Dying" from his hospital bed. "Pro: People are nicer to you. Con: You die at the end. Pro: For once the funeral doesn't interfere with your schedule. Con: After that your schedule's pretty dead. Pro: Not really worried about the ozone layer. Con: No Victoria's Secret catalogs."

Eighteen months after Joel's diagnosis, I was looking at our children, ages eleven, nine, and eight, trying to find the words to tell them that Daddy had died. Our youngest, Rachel, wrote a poem: "How will I live without him? Life was so fun, but now it's so dim." Our home was like a body without a soul. I couldn't sleep, so I stayed up talking on the phone with Joel's brothers, then reading until two or three in the morning. This went on for over a year.

One of the first books I read was *Savage Inequalities* by Jonathan Kozol, a searing rebuke of our nation's educational system. Kozol described children trapped in failing schools. And in *Amazing Grace*, he wrote about a girl who told him, "They give us the very worst schools anyone could think of."[1]

Through camp, then college, and now again: Education was what I kept returning to. I could not stop thinking about the children in Kozol's books. And their mothers. Eventually, I came across a passage in Viktor Frankl's *Man's Search for Meaning*: "It did not really matter what we expected from life, but rather what life expected from us." I took this admonition to heart. This was what life expected from me: to start a school.

My friends were quick to tell me that the idea was insane, that I wasn't thinking clearly. "It's not the right time," they said. "You have no security." My plan meant using all my savings, which would last only a short while. "Aren't you scared?" my friends asked. "The only thing that scares me," I replied, "is how depressed I'll be if I don't do this."

It was 2001. There were only a few charter schools in New York City and they had just opened, which meant no models, no resources, and no training programs for prospective school leaders. So I set up a start-up office in my basement, gathered a few volunteers, and went about figuring out how to open a school. I attended conferences, listened to lectures, and visited all kinds of schools: private, charter, magnet, and district. I sought out educators doing interesting work in the field, following them around for days at a time, observing their schools and asking hundreds of questions. The people I met became mentors and dear friends.

There was Larry Rosenstock, who had been principal of Cambridge Rindge and Latin and went on to found High Tech High, a charter school in San Diego. Larry talked about three kinds of integration: curricular integration through interdisciplinary projects, community-school integration through internships, and socioeconomic integration—which in the case of High Tech High meant a lottery system that accepted half of the students from lower- and half from upper-income neighborhoods. His schools were a national model of project-based learning, and many charter founders made the pilgrimage to San Diego to learn from him and what he was doing. "Understanding derives from creating," he would say. Years later, I would bring my children to visit him, and he would regale us with stories about the great natural scientist E. O. Wilson, who had supported his students with a conservation project.[2] Years later still, his daughter would become a kindergarten teacher at HVA, where she would meet her future husband.

There was Howard Fuller, founder of the Black Alliance for Educational Options, who had been the Milwaukee schools superintendent, a professor and civil rights activist, and a charter school advocate and founder. Howard was fearless about taking on the educational establishment. As keynote speaker at a national education conference, he electrified the audience with his stirring oratory and unapologetic defense of parental choice. "I believe deep in my heart," he said, "that giving low-income and working-class parents the power and the money to make choices about the schools their children attend will revolutionize education."[3]

There was Dennis Littky, founder of The Met, a charter school in Providence, Rhode Island. Touring his school, I was taken with how respected students were, and how focused and comfortable. Dennis had been an educational innovator since the late 1960s, when he'd added a farm at the back of his school "to teach kids how to persevere" and created one of the country's first advisory systems, long before they became popular, to provide each student with "a personal connection to a caring adult." He was among the charter founders who worked six or seven days a week, twelve hours a day. "You can see how fucking hard it is, man," he said. Yes, I could.

There was Don Shalvey, one of the early architects of the charter movement. The charter school concept was based on three principles: Parents should be able to choose their children's schools; educators should be accountable for learning outcomes; and schools should be free from bureaucratic constraints.[4] Don had been a guidance counselor, principal, and superintendent before founding the second charter school in the country and the very first in California.[5] He had pioneered the concept of a charter network—a group of schools managed by a central office, similar to a school district—and had founded Aspire, the nation's first such network.[6] Don, who was the go-to advisor for the first wave of charter school founders, allowed me to shadow him for a week. As we walked through his schools, he talked about curriculum and instruction, real estate and operations, policy and politics. We sat in his Silicon Valley office as he sketched out enrollment projections and financial models on a whiteboard. He took me to local city council meetings in communities where he was seeking permission to open new schools. We were on the road for hours each day, stopping at one point to visit his mother and at another to pick fruit in his backyard orchard. By the end of that magical week, Don had given me a crash course in school start-up. And he had me believing that it was possible to fix the entire educational system.

Then there was Geoff Canada, the inspiring leader of the Harlem Children's Zone. Geoff had galvanized leaders in New

York to support underserved families in Harlem. His concept was to provide comprehensive services from birth through adulthood to afford opportunity for children of color in low-income neighborhoods. He invited me to visit his Saturday program where experts in child development met with expectant and new moms. In his presence one couldn't help but feel moved by his idealism. Geoff encouraged me to focus on Harlem. In 2000, only 13 percent of the neighborhood's eighth graders were proficient in math; only 22 percent in reading.[7] There was a real need for quality schools in Harlem, he said.

My hope for this new school was to craft a pedagogical vision comparable with the country's finest private schools. I was especially attracted to Sidwell Friends in Washington, DC. When I visited, it was clear why presidents have sent their children there. Sidwell believed in critical thinking, unhurried reflection, and intellectual inquiry; they valued simplicity, empathy, and service. Their ethos was based on the Quaker belief that there is "that of God" in every person—a phrase that I interpreted as goodness and infinite potential. Everything about the school radiated a commitment to academic excellence. This was the quality of education that I wanted for my own children. I wanted the same for the children of Harlem.

To get started on all this, the founding lead teachers and I created a number of core structures. These included a "higher level learning rubric" with benchmarks for things like student discourse, complex questioning, and students taking ownership of their learning. We designed criteria for student behavior, preparation, and effort that we titled "self-discipline." And we established a school motto: "I am the leader of my life." But while my commitment to these ideals was firm, I did not yet have concrete systems to fully implement them.

One thing I did know was that actualizing our vision would require amazing teachers. I sifted through hundreds of resumes for every candidate who got a phone call, let alone an interview. I was looking for teachers who were brilliant but humble, always wanting feedback to learn and improve. Teachers who were passionate about academic excellence. When students find themselves in the presence of adults who have followed their calling into the classroom, they can't help but come alive to their own passion for learning.

One of the first such teachers I recruited was Rebecca Glick, who had started in a suburban school and went on to teach in Dorchester, Massachusetts, a lower-income community. When I visited Rebecca's school, most of the classrooms were chaotic, with screaming and unruly students. But not hers. Walking into Rebecca's room was like entering a magic fairyland, with students working independently, books everywhere, and a tranquil atmosphere of quiet concentration. Rebecca was leading an impressive discussion about poetry.

In addition to intellectual sophistication, I looked for teachers with a positive spirit, the kind of people who responded to problems by jumping in and figuring out how to solve them. I sought out individuals who cared so much about their students and, by extension, their school that they never wanted to miss a day so as not to burden their colleagues or abandon their kids. I looked for self-driven people who cared about excellence, who regarded student arrival and dismissal not as assigned "duties" but as a great opportunity to connect with parents. In other words, I looked for individuals who already shared my vision and values.

We said that our children came first, and we meant it. We *wanted* to go above and beyond for them. The school day ran from 7:30 to 4:30, then we offered tutoring and homework help until 5:30. Many teachers would arrive early, leave late, or both, often staying until 6:30 or 7:00 to tutor students, call parents, compare notes, and make sure their classrooms were tidy and sparkling. Others would work at home, often until as late as 10:00, refining their lesson plans. We made ourselves available for students to call until 9:00 if they had homework questions. After the end of each year, we held a leadership retreat to debrief and work on improvements for the next year. Then we would get ready for our five-week professional-development institute for teachers. On summer evenings, after a full day's work, our principals and teachers would visit new students at home to build relationships with them and their families, who appreciated the personal attention and kindness. We believed that self-sacrifice was necessary to properly serve our students.

My life revolved around my own three children and our schoolchildren. Tuesday nights were faculty meetings for immediate problem-solving; Thursday nights, at Patsy's in East Harlem, were leadership meetings for advance planning. Saturday mornings we ran tutoring for students who needed remediation (my kids came in to help), and on Sunday afternoons we had conference calls about issues that required lengthier discussions. Once a month, we stayed at school for several nights poring over assessments for data-driven instructional planning. Winter vacation was our four-day continual improvement retreat. We felt energized by one another.

Our optimism, ingenuity, and relentless obsession with excellence extended to every facet of school life. That included attendance, which was consistently at 98 percent or better—even during a transit strike. Yohana, our founding office manager, dean, and family-engagement coordinator all in one, spent the entire night organizing carpools. We were meticulous about continually refining every detail of our schools. Among other things, we designed a rapid-response daily data system to precisely target individual learning gaps so students wouldn't fall behind for even a day. What a difference it can make in a child's life when schools are filled with a dedicated team eager to go the extra mile to help them.

We were unified in our disdain for complacency and bureaucracy, both of which were pervasive in many of the public schools where our teachers had previously worked. We could not abide complaining, gossiping, mediocrity, self-centeredness, arrogance, negativity, or divisiveness. We talked about these as "DOE" (Department of Education) culture. Instead, we had a wonderful esprit de corps, the sort that comes from being kind and trustworthy and assuming the best of one another: that feeling you have when you walk out of a room and know that your colleagues won't start talking about you behind your back.

"I think the students can sense that we're all a little bit in love with each other," one teacher said.

We could all sense that we were part of something incredibly special. We saw HVA not as a career but as a life's work, a sacred mission. People would say that you could *feel* the great vibes when you walked inside our schools.

In our first five years, all this was organic. As we grew larger, we became more purposeful about naming our values—children first, holding ourselves accountable, respecting teachers, trust and kindness—and continually striving to sustain our culture.

Our most important resource in all this was love. There is a saying that "words that come from the heart enter the heart." Children can intuit how you feel about them. It's not a technique; it's caring about your students. This is why we hired people who genuinely loved kids: teachers who chose to spend their Saturdays at a school picnic or planting a garden with students or going to their football games to cheer them on.

That love embraced our families as well. The month we opened, Yohana and I organized a series of potluck dinners for parents, students, and teachers. Potlucks—not pizza. The mothers were proud to bring their favorite pasta or rice recipes. "I'm bringing my famous brownies!" one grandmother said. Sharing food naturally brought us closer together.

And instead of one potluck for the whole school, we held six of them to keep the groups small, which allowed us to really get to know our families and create close relationships. We sent home invitations with the children, made follow-up calls, then more calls, and we ended up with 100 percent attendance at all six evenings.

Yohana and I chatted with the parents as they arrived. I asked as many of them as possible what they felt was going well in school and what they thought we needed to improve. After only half an hour, I had more than five pages of notes, which we followed up on in the weeks ahead.

Once we finished eating, I asked the parents, grandparents, and guardians to sit in the chairs that we had arranged in a circle and the children to sit on the floor in front of us. Then I invited the adults to stand. I took the hands of the parents to my left and right and asked everyone else to do the same. The simple act of standing in a circle holding hands changed the feeling of our school. The families appreciated that we weren't a typical big-city public school giving them a PowerPoint presentation in a cavernous, impersonal auditorium.

As our students looked up at their families, standing around them all holding hands in a circle, I spoke from the heart. "Look around," I said. "Eight years from now when you go off to college, you will think back on this day. All of us together—your family, your classmates, and me and your teachers—we are one big family. We are here to love and support you. We will be here for you no matter what. Now, you have responsibilities, too. We expect a lot from you. We expect you to behave and listen to your teachers. We expect you to do all of your homework, all of it, every night. We expect you to take your classwork seriously. We will not let you get away with second-rate work, because you are capable of excellence."

Several parents started tearing up. "For the first time, I don't feel alone," one mother whispered to me. We were a community now, and we would raise these children together.

Public schools often blame parents for not being involved. But we made it *our* responsibility to involve families. And to treat them with the respect they deserved. We established that our families should feel like guests at the Ritz-Carlton when they visited the school. For example, we said that when any staff member sees a parent on the premises, they should greet them with a warm smile and proactively ask, "Are you being helped?"

There was a direct connection between our culture of caring and the high bar we set for academics. We insisted on excellence because we believed in the students, in their ability, and they sensed that. Since we opened with fifth grade, our students came to us after six years at failing public schools, some of the worst in the city. They entered about four years behind, some at a kindergarten or first-grade level, as their former schools had often failed to teach them how to add or subtract single-digit numbers or read simple words. If they didn't do their homework, they said, no one noticed, no one cared. "I used to throw my books away," one boy said.

We needed to catch our students up on all the learning they had missed, but we also needed to address their self-perception. Because their prior schools had expected so little of them, they had gotten the message that they were not capable. We immediately sent the opposite message. We not only assigned two hours of homework each night; we also followed through consistently to make sure that it was done and done well. We did not accept anything less than complete work. We focused relentlessly on learning outcomes; if a student didn't understand something, we would get them into tutoring the same day or, at the latest, the next week. All this had a direct impact on the way our students saw themselves. "The school believed in me, then I started to believe in myself," a sixth-grade girl said.

Victoria was a special education student in our very first class. One day, her mother had taken me aside. "We were told by her old school to be realistic," she'd said. "Realistic about what?" I asked. "Not to expect her to graduate from high school." It was unconscionable, yet it was typical of the disrespect toward families of color at so many public schools, not to mention the utter lack of accountability. At our school, Victoria thrived. A few years later, her mom became seriously ill. Knowing that she didn't have much time left, she took me aside again. "The public school system almost had me convinced that my little girl would be nothing. They almost had me. We both know better. Please look after my baby. Your school is a blessing." As I worked in our schools every day, my heart and mind were focused on children like Victoria (and yes, she *did* graduate from high school)—the life their families wanted for them, the way their families entrusted us with their education, the kind of schools they deserved.

But progress did not come easily. Our students' former schools had also failed to teach them to comport themselves respectfully in class. For many, the default mode was to slouch, space out, mumble, fidget, and disrupt. “I tossed bottles out the windows,” one boy said. “All the kids did it.” More than anything, our students talked about the constant fighting in their old schools. “There were fights in the halls, fights in class, fighting every day,” one girl told Yohana. “Nobody cared about me.” Another said she hid in the bathroom during lunch to avoid the fights. A little boy told me that he'd seen another student stabbed. Another said, “Kids are mean. Kids fight and hurt you. But it's no big deal.”

No big deal. These children were being desensitized to violence at an early age. They were being robbed of their childhood.

I had seen it firsthand. Back when I conducted field research in preparation for founding HVA, I visited big city schools in the South Bronx, Newark, East Harlem, the Roxbury neighborhood in Boston, and the South Side of Chicago. Police were everywhere: at the entrance, in the halls, in the cafeteria. It's almost impossible to fathom how severely the school system had neglected the children I saw in these schools. Students were running through the halls, jumping on desks, throwing sharp pencils at teachers, mocking teachers, refusing to work, talking through lessons, sleeping during lessons. The chaos in their former schools, as our students told us when they came to HVA, made it hard if not impossible to learn.

In response, many schools had designed disciplinary systems with elaborate infrastructures of prizes and punishments, points and demerits—all to produce obedience. But in solving one problem, they had created another: the systematic undermining of student agency, that is, the capacity to be self-directed. If students aren't allowed to develop agency, they will be relegated to the underclass.

When I asked the principal of one such school about her philosophy on student behavior, she replied: "We do whatever works." *Works to accomplish what?* I thought. Given my disdain for mindless compliance, I was dubious about this.

I had seen chaotic schools, and I had seen safe but regimented schools that micromanage students. Were these the only options? I didn't like either.

So, in thinking through the issue of behavior as we prepared to open our doors, I went back to my core idea: Our new school in Harlem must be best in class, and that included cultivating a moral compass in our students. To be sure, I believed in consequences for misbehavior. But good behavior alone was not enough. We didn't want to teach kids to behave simply to avoid a consequence or win a prize. I would never have said to my own children, "If you're polite to the UPS guy, I'll give you a quarter." I believed in teaching children to be kind and gracious, to do the right thing *because* it's the right thing.

We therefore took a risk and, contrary to the advice of everyone I had met during my year of field research, we opened our school without a system of prizes and demerits.

Then reality hit. The first week of school was a mess. Almost every class was sending several students out each day for disrespect. The dean's office was overflowing. Rebecca's class was the exception; she had her students behaving remarkably well no matter what was going on around them. But, for the most part, students were being sent out for misbehavior every hour.

It went on like that for months. Finally, just before Thanksgiving, Rebecca pulled me aside. "I understand how strongly you feel," she said, "and you know I agree philosophically, but the school needs either demerits—or something."

Or something. The problem was that I had nothing else to offer, no system that was both aligned with my philosophy and had any chance to work.

At last, we decided to institute demerits. We had already set up very strict rules regarding every single detail of student behavior—no getting out of your seat without permission, no slouching, no speaking out of turn, no disrespect of any kind. The demerits also covered preparation, organization, timely arrival, completion of homework with best effort, and more. Now, when students broke a rule, they earned a demerit. Three demerits meant detention. Egregious disrespect would earn more serious consequences. Each Friday, we sent home a report so that parents would be kept apprised of their child's behavior, preparation, effort, and homework.

I reluctantly agreed to this system, but with three conditions. First, we would not give prizes for good behavior. Second, we would emphatically reject a rigid or demeaning culture; our school would continue to feel like a loving community that respected children and childhood. Third, importantly, the system would be temporary. We were only in our first year. We would figure out a better way.

We immediately started trying. Over the summer, we worked

to design behavioral routines—protocols for how to participate in a class discussion, how to respond to teacher directions, how to enter and exit the classroom respectfully—that we began to teach during the first few weeks of the year. When students practice routines and teachers uphold them consistently, students internalize them to the point that they become second nature.

After an immense amount of work, behavior improved. Students said they felt happy and safe and protected. They no longer held the anxiety that comes from having to keep up a tough exterior. They could enjoy their childhood. One mother said to me: "My child is a child again."

Just as we took a different, more aspirational approach to school culture, so, too, we took a different approach to academics. In teaching reading, for example, many schools I visited did not engage students in sustained reading. Instead, they were given worksheets, so they just skimmed books to find the answers.

I believe that children need to be avid readers in order to become intellectually sophisticated, so I told our teachers that our goal was for our students to love reading. If we could get students to genuinely love reading, I said, they would naturally read a lot, like an hour a day, and that would add up to about fifty books a year. I gave only one guideline: no points or prizes. We started with a half hour of uninterrupted reading time in class each day to get them hooked, and then we added an expectation of another thirty minutes of reading at home each night, plus an hour or more per day on the weekends. But the expectation was not the point. We wanted students to want to read. We created inviting classroom libraries stocked with high-quality books, and we gave students choice over their book selections. (This was in addition to the required reading in English class.) We got to know their personal interests up front so we could recommend good books on those topics, then conferred with them regularly to find out more about them as readers. We taught them to write book recommendations and lead book talks for their classmates. We read aloud the first pages of great books to get the kids hooked, so that they would want to read the rest on their own.

Later I came across *The Reading Zone*, a book by Nancie Atwell filled with ideas for how to develop students into avid readers. Atwell had quoted one of her students describing how it feels to be immersed in a good book: "It's hard to explain," he said. "I'm in the book. I forget where I am. I don't notice that I'm turning the pages. Time goes by incredibly fast. Everything around me disappears. I don't want to stop reading."[8] This was precisely what we wanted for our students, to be "in the zone"—to be flashlight-under-the-covers, intrinsically motivated readers. Teachers and even students talked about selecting books that would put you in the zone, and I ran an optional Friday meeting to study the ideas in *The Reading Zone* and for teachers to share their ideas for how to continually improve our work in that regard. And we made reading into a whole-school project: Not just reading teachers but everyone from science and math teachers to the office manager and security staff would contribute ideas and talk about books with the kids. Reading became the cornerstone of our academic culture. Students who told us they had not previously read more than one or two books a year were now reading fifty. The sheer volume had a dramatic impact on their comprehension, knowledge, vocabulary, and intellectual power.

We approached math differently as well. I had read in *The Teaching Gap* about Japanese math instruction, a problem-based approach that develops students' deep understanding through intellectual struggle, and I hired educators who shared my philosophy. I disagreed with the methods that were ubiquitous in urban schools: teaching math through songs, chants, and memorization gimmicks. We also disagreed with the "I do, we do, you do" approach, in which teachers describe a procedure at the beginning of a lesson and students memorize it through repetitive practice but don't necessarily understand what it means or why it matters. Instead, from our very first year, we taught math using problem-based instruction. Each lesson started with students grappling with a problem for a sustained period of time, and only then did the teacher lead them through a process of guided thinking to get at the underlying principle the problem exemplified. Our approach led to deep conceptual understanding. "The essence of mathematics," Paul Lockhart says, "is learning how to devise solutions to problems, not memorizing solutions devised by someone else."[9]

One of our first eighth-grade math teachers, Peter Coe, was a Yale math major and Teach for America alum. Peter would eventually go on to help design the math curriculum and assessments for New York State. "Before I came to HVA, I thought I knew how to teach math," he said years later. "HVA transformed the way I teach."

Although our students continued to enter as fifth graders many years behind grade level, we were producing sky-high test scores. By 2007, HVA ranked number one in eighth-grade math among public schools in New York State and surpassed the district, city, and state averages by substantial margins in reading as well. The next year, we achieved 100 percent proficiency in math (compared to 32 percent in Harlem district schools).[10] After we opened our high school, 100 percent of our students passed all state Regents Exams required for graduation (compared to 38 percent in Harlem).[11] Families were delighted. Visitors were blown away by the excellent behavior and attentiveness of our students and by the passion of our teachers. Our schools were becoming known for an intellectual culture. "I was mesmerized," one new teacher said. "I had never experienced a workplace with so many dazzling ideas, personalities, and authentic excitement." HVA was cherished in Harlem as "a source of great pride" and "an important part of our community."[12] In the spring of our fourth year, 2007, HVA was selected to receive a visit from the president of the United States. "I love coming to a place where people defy expectations," President Bush said.[13] In 2009, US Secretary of Education Arne Duncan said, "We need more schools like Harlem Village Academies."[14] That same year, Mayor Mike

Bloomberg called Harlem Village Academies "the poster child for this country" and declared January 12 HVA Day in New York City.[15] In 2010, *Oprah Magazine* called our schools "revolutionary,"[16] and in 2011, *Time* magazine lauded HVA's "cooperative critical spirit" of accountability.[17] We were regularly referred to as one of the highest-performing schools in the country.

But the accolades just exacerbated my discontent. It's one thing to refer to schools as high performing; it's another to examine what that means. I wanted so much more for our students than excellent behavior and test scores. It was a delicate balancing act to ensure that our teachers knew how much I appreciated their hard work while still pushing all of us further. I would open our annual summer institute with a speech about my vision. "The whole country is astounded by what you have accomplished, and I am so proud of you," I said one year. "The world looks at our test scores and says we've closed the achievement gap. But we know better. We measure achievement by how well our students can analyze a text, solve complex problems, write coherently."

Each year, we steadily worked our way toward higher and higher levels of learning—but it was slow going. Some of our teaching was mind-blowing, with cognitively demanding questions and challenging academic tasks—but it was not consistent. And each year it seemed to get harder to swim against the tide. New teachers came to our schools, bright and talented but trained to manage behavior with clapping, snapping, countdowns. These techniques were easy to deploy but contrary to what we believed about good teaching. We also waged a constant battle against worksheets. As for the demerit system, it was still in place; we hadn't been able to figure out an alternative.

On top of all this, perhaps the biggest obstacle was time. There was never enough time to both fully pursue our vision *and* help students to catch up on all the learning they had missed before joining us in fifth grade. Providing the intensive support they needed for remediation took an inordinate amount of time—before school, after school, on weekends and vacations, in the summer—all of our time, really.

I was working late one afternoon when a colleague bounded into my office. "The scores came in," he said. "We're outperforming almost everyone again, even Scarsdale and some Upper East Side schools. And we beat Chappaqua!"

Chappaqua is among the most affluent suburban districts in the country, on par with the best private schools. I knew the quality of student thinking that the schools there produced. In my view, we were not doing better than Chappaqua. Not even close.

When I tried to explain this to people, I'd take out a piece of paper and draw a box. Inside, at the top, I'd write "HVA." "Look," I'd say, "every year the state says we rank at the top, here. If this is all you see, being on top is great." Then I would draw a second box above the first. "But there is another world we should measure ourselves against," I'd say, pointing to it. "This is where the elite suburban schools like Chappaqua and

Scarsdale are. This is where the private schools like Sidwell Friends are. *This is where our students deserve to be.*"

Schools in Chappaqua, Scarsdale, schools like Sidwell Friends: They did not define achievement as good behavior and passing state tests. They believed that schools should prepare students, as the Sidwell Friends brochure said, to "analyze, question, critique, and interpret information and ideas." They saw it as their responsibility to "nurture a person rooted as much in the unseen as in the seen." My dream was for our children in Harlem to receive a world-class education on par with such a grand vision. To me it was glaringly obvious, all evidence to the contrary notwithstanding, that we had not yet accomplished this.

3.

The Beauty and Difficulty of the Task

About ten years after we started our schools, a colleague asked to meet. "We need to share our best practices," he said. "All the other schools are sharing their best practices." Yes, yes. I knew all the others were doing this. But I just couldn't. I didn't want to share practices that I knew were not "best." (I did not think the practices that others were sharing were best, either, but that was beside the point.)

"Why are you never satisfied?" he asked. But what I genuinely did not understand was how anyone *could* be satisfied with our schools as they were. I was reaching a breaking point. I felt dejected, achingly disappointed that I had not yet been able to produce the consistently exquisite education that I had envisioned. I was, as Robert Gottlieb once said, unhappy with myself and in myself.

So in the summer of 2012, I assessed my life. I needed to find my bearings. To read. And to think. After the last day of school, instead of my usual routine of planning for the upcoming year, I took a few weeks to disconnect from the day-to-day. I found myself turning to some of the books that I'd read in college: Ginsberg, Emerson, Rilke's *Letters to a Young Poet*. Thus began what I came to think of as my summer of existential crisis.

While I didn't know what to do, I did have the clarity of my convictions. All I could do was stay resolute. I relied on Rilke. "We know little, but that we must hold to what is difficult is a certainty that will not forsake us."

I called Rebecca, our stellar founding teacher, who had just moved to Hong Kong. I told her about my dissatisfaction. In response, she repeated something she had said all those years ago, back when we'd first met. "You're trying to do the schools nobody thinks can be done." But this time she added, "You're halfway there."

Perhaps, I said, but I did not think that slow and steady would get us the rest of the way. We had to go *all in*. That's what I had been thinking: all in. We had to go further, faster. "Okay," Rebecca said, "then do what you always do: Gather the smartest people. I'm not talking about the best teachers; I'm talking about the people *they* look up to, the people whose books they have read. Find the master teachers of the master teachers."

She was right. I would start by gathering a group of the best educational minds in the country.

I made a short list of the educators whose ideas I most respected, whose books I'd read repeatedly—kept in a stack on my desk, marked up with highlights and underlines and Post-its. These individuals, for the most part, were not known in the charter community, but in mainstream education circles they were icons. Whenever I explained my educational vision, these were the books I referred to in meetings, distributed at leadership retreats, quoted in speeches.

There was Grant Wiggins's *Understanding by Design*, an education classic.[1] Grant was an internationally respected authority on curriculum and assessment. His core concepts—backward design (the idea that curricula should be reverse engineered from big ideas and desired performance outcomes) and essential questions (the notion that the questions teachers ask should be meaningful and provoke deep thinking about important issues)—were de rigueur in almost every high school in America (although, as Grant would later explain, they were usually not understood or implemented well).

There was *Shades of Meaning*, by Donna Santman, about literacy instruction and the quality of student thinking. One of Donna's areas of expertise was student discourse. "The silence that surrounds kids as they search their minds for words to explain their ideas often feels deafening," she wrote. "It's incredibly tempting to fill that void."[2] Donna explained that teachers need to resist the urge to do all the talking and instead teach students to articulate their thinking.

There was *An Ethic of Excellence*, by Ron Berger. A veteran educator of thirty-eight years, Ron was chief academic officer of EL Education, a curriculum and professional development nonprofit, and a friend of Larry, the founder of High Tech

High. Ron's central passion was student work, particularly the use of models—exemplary essays, lab reports, scientific drawings, and so on—to promote effective feedback, revision, and thus learning. "Rather than seeing school as something being done to them," Ron wrote, students should be given "responsibility to carry out original academic projects, display their work, and reflect publicly on their work and their learning."[3]

And then there was Shelley Harwayne. Shelley had been the founder and principal of the Manhattan New School, a public school that was so exceptional it was seen as being on the level of elite private schools. She went on to become superintendent of New York City's District 2, known for its world-class professional development.[4] Shelley's many books included *Going Public*, which was chock-full of the wisdom she had gleaned from nearly a decade of running her school. I had highlighted it three times in three different colors.[5]

While I did not know any of these educational luminaries, I hoped they might be willing to meet and, ideally, form a think tank of sorts. So I made some calls and began a series of meetings, first with each of them individually.

Shelley came to visit us at one of our newly opened elementary schools. In her late sixties, she crouched down spryly next to our five-year-olds to talk with them and watch them work. She knew more than all of us combined, and she knew exactly what to ask the children in order to evaluate the school: "Can you tell me about your work? Why did the teacher ask you to do what you're doing? What are you supposed to do if you're having trouble?" As we left the classroom, she explained that students, even in kindergarten, should be able to articulate the purpose of their work, an indicator that the instruction is fostering independence and metacognition. "It's *so interesting* . . ." she kept saying—referring to things she clearly thought we were not doing well.

Donna met with me at one of our middle schools. I invited her to walk through our classrooms. When we sat down afterward, she was clear as can be: "The teachers are doing most of the talking. Whoever is doing the talking in the classroom is doing the thinking." I was energized by this critique. It immediately resonated. "Speaking is a mediator for thinking"—this would become one of my favorite Donna-isms.

Grant traveled up to Harlem as well. I shared my disagreement with the pedagogical methods in urban schools and asked him for his thoughts. "I agree," he said. "It's a real problem. And it's been getting worse." I also shared my impatience with our slow pace of progress. "Cut yourself a break," he said. "You can't accomplish this in a few years or even twenty years. This is a life's work, *generational work*. We have to be in it for the long game."[6] Grant was advising private schools in Paris and New York that, he said, were working on many of the same things that we were trying to do. We ended up talking for hours. By the end, Grant said that he wanted to be an integral part of our project. "You want this to be state-of-the-art education," he said. "I'm in!"

Ron came to see me at our new high school. Like Grant and me, Ron was concerned about the pedagogy in urban public education. "It's not at all my vision," he said. "It scares me." He added that schools were approaching classroom management as if it were crisis management. Later, we continued our discussion over dinner. He talked about his childhood and family, his early years as a teacher, his work on passion-driven arts education with Yo-Yo Ma. Toward the end of the evening, I showed him a one-pager that summarized our proposed new assessment system. "It has all the components," he said. "But there is a larger point. The power of the system is not the system itself. The power is in the never-ending discussion about quality that the system inspires." (This reminded me of a master yoga teacher who had said, "The purpose of yoga is not the postures. The postures are a conduit for the breath.") Ron said that schools need a culture where teachers are continually talking about quality, seeking to understand quality, pushing for improved quality. "What is a quality lesson? What is quality student work?"

Our nascent merry band of educators continued to grow. We recruited Monique Knight from Teachers College, where she had been a literacy specialist. Monique became a mentor teacher in one of our kindergartens (Larry's daughter would later be one of her mentees). I was captivated by her talent. Her classroom was the very model of my vision, with children engrossed in learning activities they had each selected, singing between activities, and walking around with the look of confident joy that we had seen in private school kindergartens. It was Montessori-esque—and quite the opposite of the worksheets and drills we had seen in so many urban kindergartens.

While Monique and others in the group were steeped in

elementary literacy, BC Craig brought expertise in teacher education and social studies. BC had been a social studies teacher for a decade before becoming a professor at Bard College. She was exceptionally knowledgeable about what comprises great teaching. When one of our English teachers heard that we would be speaking with BC, she took it upon herself to email our high school principal. "BC was the best professor I had in grad school," she wrote. "She is brilliant! No other professor, class, or mentor prepared me as much as BC." We would soon find that this was what everyone said about her.

Shelley became the group's informal leader. She was a mentor to the mentors to the mentors. "I've spent my entire career trying to learn from and be like Shelley," Donna said. Shelley introduced us to some of the master teachers from her days at the Manhattan New School, including Sharon Taberski, an influential literacy expert, and Kevin Tallat-Kelpsa, whom I immediately recognized as a kindred spirit. Kevin had gone on to be a coach of math coaches across New York City. Whereas most master teachers were experts in one academic area, Kevin was the rare talent who had expertise in several. On top of that, his work ethic and sense of urgency were unparalleled and a perfect match with our values. Shelley said Kevin reminded her of herself when she was a new principal. I asked Kevin to join us, and he soon became a principal and then a mentor to other principals.

After a few rounds of individual meetings, we began to work together as a group. Grant suggested that we focus on curriculum first. "We need a shared definition of what we mean by curriculum," he said. As our curriculum go-to guy, he took the lead. We gathered in a circle in an elementary classroom, and he opened by saying that even after all these years, curriculum is still misunderstood. "A curriculum should not start by listing topics to cover. It needs to be framed around big ideas." Grant described his backward-design approach to curriculum, and the group talked about how to ensure that questions and topics across all grade levels are meaningful. "When I was superintendent and walked into a classroom," Shelley said, "if I didn't have the urge to enter the conversation, then I thought it's not compelling enough for the kids. They should be learning about things that matter."

Our next round of meetings concentrated on instruction and assessment. We sat in a circle again, this time in my office, and covered the walls with chart paper. "We need students writing not just short responses but extended essays," Grant said. "And teachers asking questions that move students into deeper levels of thinking," Donna added. Kevin talked about students grappling with complex problems. Sharon talked about the purposeful use of space. As a first-grade teacher, she had designed the physical setup of her classroom to foster independence, including placing paper, folders, and supplies at kindergarten eye level, teaching the little ones how to access and organize supplies rather than doing that work for them, and using furniture to divide the room into smaller spaces so students could manage on their own. She'd learned all this from Reggio Emilia, an educational approach developed in

Italy that teaches that, when set up properly, classroom design can be so helpful that it's like an extra teacher guiding children to be independent.[7] All these concepts resonated with me. I could barely contain my excitement.

As the group spent more time together, I noticed a couple of things. First, although they were each exceedingly knowledgeable, they exhibited an eagerness to learn and felt honored to be in one another's company. Second, although they had not originally known one another, had come from different backgrounds, and had different areas of specialization, they all had a similar perspective on education. They were part of a lineage, a tradition. They shared a common language, common beliefs, a fabric of knowledge about teaching and learning.

The idea of tradition has always intrigued me: the idea of standing in relation to people who came before us and to those who will come after. The idea of humility and reverence for wisdom. The idea that things of value and beauty—philosophy, religion, literature, music—are studied and emulated as they evolve through the generations.

As I listened to the group talking about the people they respected, I thought of Jimi Hendrix being transfixed and influenced by Muddy Waters. I thought of the poets and singer-songwriters in the coffeehouses of 1950s and '60s Greenwich Village. "You just watched and tried to pick up the essence of what they were doing," Bob Dylan said.[8] I thought of the Beatles' *Rubber Soul* inspiring Brian Wilson to write "God Only Knows," then Wilson's *Pet Sounds* inspiring the Beatles to write *Sgt. Pepper*. I thought of Talmudic scholars who, before articulating lines of reasoning, proofs and counterproofs, begin their commentary by crediting multiple generations of predecessors ("Rabbi So-and-So learned from Rabbi So-and-So who learned from Rabbi So-and-So . . .").

In the same way, our master educators often talked about the people *they* had learned from. Larry spoke about Bob Moses, the civil rights activist and educator who, in 1982, founded the Algebra Project (and had been Larry's seventh-grade math teacher). Shelley spoke about Donald Graves, who revolutionized writing instruction in the 1970s. Sharon spoke about Jerome Bruner, the cognitive psychologist whose 1956 book, *A Study of Thinking*, transformed our understanding of the mind. Grant spoke often of Ralph Tyler's approach to curriculum from the 1940s. And the educators that Grant, Larry—everyone, really—seemed to speak about the most were Ted Sizer and Debbie Meier.[9]

Ted was arguably the most influential American educator of the second half of the twentieth century. After starting as a teacher at the Roxbury Latin School in 1955, he became the youngest ever dean of the Harvard School of Education, then head of school at Andover for a decade. It was there that he began to think about the entrenched, ineffectual structures of American schools. This reflection led him to undertake a five-year study that resulted in his landmark book, *Horace's Compromise*, and to his creation of the Coalition of Essential Schools in 1983.[10] Dennis Littky's Met School was the first member of the coalition, which ultimately grew to some one thousand schools.[11] University presidents referred to Ted as a national treasure, and his influence reached generations of educators throughout the country—some of whom called themselves Ted Heads! Ted changed the national conversation. He articulated ideas—curricular depth, performance assessment, and exhibitions, to name a few—that made their way into the education zeitgeist and are still used today by thousands of schools across the country.

Debbie founded Central Park East, known as "New York's most famous public school," in 1974. Her school design was based on her experience attending Ethical Culture, a Manhattan private school. It was when she started as a teacher on the South Side of Chicago that she discovered the glaring disparity in how children were taught in low-income as opposed to affluent schools.[12] A MacArthur "genius" fellow, Debbie had written *The Power of Their Ideas*, which urged people to take seriously the concept "that every citizen is capable of the kind of intellectual competence previously attained by only a small minority."[13] She believed that the purpose of education is "to raise powerful citizens who can determine if they're being conned."[14] In 1985, Debbie formulated her famous "Habits of Mind," an elaboration of Ted's principle that schools should teach students to use their minds well. The habits include evidence (How do we know what's true or false? What evidence counts?), viewpoint (Who said it? What if you looked at it from a different direction?), connection (Is there a pattern? Have we seen something like this before?), conjecture (What if it were different?), and relevance (Who cares? Why does this matter?). Teaching these habits, she said, would "develop students as independent thinkers who are inclined to protect democracy."[15] Debbie, whom I met at an education conference in 2017, said that Ted's writings moved her to start a high school, which became the second school in his coalition.[16]

Debbie spoke frequently of John Dewey, who, she said, "wanted everyone to have a ruling-class education." Dewey was considered the father of progressive education and "the most important American public intellectual of his day."[17] Dewey himself, however, gave credit to Francis Parker, saying that *he* was the father of progressive education.[18] Shelley, Grant, Ron, and Larry were born around 1950; Howard in 1941; Debbie, Ted, and Bob Moses in the 1930s; Dewey in 1859; Parker in 1837—a legacy of wisdom stretching through the generations.

In order to deepen our work, I asked Ron to lead the group on a retreat. As we prepared, he suggested that I draft a vision statement to give to the group for their feedback—feedback, of course, being one of Ron's core concepts. I also gathered readings into a binder. On the cover, I put that famous photo of Einstein sticking out his tongue, to convey the idea of genius with a touch of rebellion. Ron proved to be an outstanding retreat leader for this group of formidable intellects. He was their peer in terms of academic experience, yet he exuded a humility and gentleness that had everyone a little bit in love with him. Ron, in turn, was enchanted by the group.

The days were intense and productive. We spent hours discussing learning theory and working to formulate plans—everyone talking, debating, the ideas flying back and forth. I drank in their words as I kept thinking about how our children in Harlem would benefit from the educational quality that would emerge from this conclave.

In the evenings, we discovered just how much we enjoyed each other's company. The first night, we played word games, laughing till our jaws hurt. The second, we sat around a campfire with guitars. I was reminded of my summers at camp.

"My whole life has been leading to this moment. I'm surrounded by brilliant people and incredible conversations. I've found my home," Kevin said. "I feel like I'm part of something larger than myself," Donna added. "We are a collective. There's all this genius around me."

After the retreat, I emailed the group a thank you note along with an excerpt from *Organizing Genius*, a book about groups of great thinkers who pursued groundbreaking work:

> Genius is rare, and the chance to exercise it in a dance with others is rarer still. The people who can achieve something truly unprecedented see things differently. They see the world not the way others believe it to be. They do not usually know what's supposed to be impossible. They are so taken with the beauty and difficulty of the task that they don't want to talk about anything else, be anywhere else, do anything else. Great groups are made

> up of people with rare gifts working together as equals. The talented smell out places that are full of promise and energy, the places where the future is being made.[19]

When we got back to school, Shelley was clear about what she thought the group ought to be doing: rolling up their sleeves, jumping in, and teaching in our classrooms alongside our teachers. She set an example by jumping in herself. Never mind that she had been a nationally acclaimed superintendent. There she was, sitting cross-legged on the floor in the middle of a class of second graders, demonstrating what great instruction looks and sounds like. Surrounded by twenty teachers observing her intently, Shelley started reading to the kids. The way she did so, drawing them into the ideas in the book by speaking to them in a gentle, inviting tone and at a high intellectual level, could not have been more different from the hyperactive and formulaic approach that young teachers are so often trained to use. She engaged the students with meaningful observations and challenging questions, pausing organically to give them time to think and react.

Shelley would work a full day without so much as a lunch break—"I'll just have this egg salad sandwich, and I'll get back to classrooms in ten minutes." "Leadership means being in the classrooms," she'd say. That was one of the Shelley-isms we loved. Another was "The main thing is to keep the main thing the main thing," which meant that quality instruction is what matters most and you can't get distracted by the hundreds of other tasks involved in running a school. Like us, she believed in accountability and always putting children first. "As superintendent," she said, "I would ask my principals: 'Would you put your child in this class?' If not, then it's not good enough for anyone else's kids."

The other mentors followed Shelley's lead and jumped into our classrooms as well. This, to me, was the real genius: the coming together of these veterans with bright, energetic teachers. Melissa Black, for instance, an exceptional kindergarten teacher, said that she learned from Sharon Taberski how to teach the youngest students to self-monitor their learning. "Sharon taught me that when students are struggling, the teacher should not step in and do the work for them but carefully watch and guide them," Melissa said. "If I'm teaching first graders about long vowels and short vowels, I will teach them directly. Then they will practice by reading out loud. When students make a mistake, like saying a short *e* instead of a long *e*, my natural response would have been to just correct them. But based on what I learned from Sharon, I point to the letter and ask them to reread and self-correct."

Superb teaching was starting to emerge in classrooms like Melissa's. "HVA kept me from becoming a Pinterest teacher," she said. "I learned that excellent instruction is about students creating quality work. That kept me from doing the shallow, cutesy lesson plans on Pinterest that pass for instruction."

The mentors' influence was also beginning to permeate our academic culture in more subtle but still powerful ways. In our middle schools, for example, Donna taught protocols for student-owned discourse. Sitting in a circle with students, each with a book in hand, she would say to them: "You know it's your turn to talk when nobody else is talking." This shifted their mindset from that of passively waiting until a teacher called on them to being intellectually engaged learners, intently listening to one another's ideas and taking the initiative to join the classroom discourse.

While all this was going on, I was leading a recursive learning process that connected the group's work to the daily improvement of teaching and learning in our schools. In tackling a given topic—say, demonstrating application of knowledge and skills through performance assessment—I would start by meeting with the group. On weekends, I'd read whatever they had recommended. Next, I'd synthesize the ideas I had been discussing and reading about, bring in drafts of protocols or initiatives on Monday, and get feedback from a principal or teacher or a group of teachers. Then we would decide how to apply the ideas in the classroom. We would reflect on the results, revise—and run the whole cycle all over again. The process continued for years as we increasingly refined our understanding.

But none of this was smooth or straightforward. We faced several challenges. For one, some of our leaders were reluctant to take risks. When we wanted to move toward student independence in our behavior systems, for instance, one colleague said that it would be way too difficult to implement. "It's too risky. The kids won't behave unless the deans are watching them."

Another challenge was the difficulty of unlearning ingrained teaching habits. Teaching conventions do not readily change because habits become the default culture, which is inordinately powerful. Teachers generally teach the way they were taught and the way they saw others teach in their novice years. In *The Teaching Gap*, Stigler and Hiebert call this the cultural code or DNA of teaching.[20]

I had also failed to establish adequate systems to help teachers implement our vision. Dan, an English teacher, was recruited away by another network. I was disappointed to lose him, and we stayed in touch. A few months into his new role, I asked how it was going. "They don't have the brilliant educational vision like at HVA. But what they do have is systems. I mean they have systems for everything. It's impressive."

Indeed, after my opening remarks at our annual summer institute one year, a seventh-grade teacher approached me. "Your call for incredible sophistication in pedagogy—your vision—it's why we're all here," he said. "But you need to be more emphatic and explicit. I mean literally spell it out: What should we do and not do?" This led to my drafting a two-page "we do, we do not" document:

We teach routines for respectful independence;
we do not use countdowns, clapping, and snapping.

We teach students to self-manage their behavior;
we do not use rewards, points, or prizes.

We use notebooks;
we do not use worksheets.

We feature student work on bulletin boards;
we do not use commercial or teacher-created displays.

We structure lessons to elicit and develop deep thinking;
we do not use PowerPoint presentations.

We engage students in meaningful work;
we do not use chants and cheers in academic settings.

The teacher who had suggested that I do this was delighted. But another disagreed with the list and decided not to return the next year. When I told Larry that I was unhappy about this, he said, "If you want to create something important and take it as far as it will go, you will lose some people, and that's okay."

This was the ultimate challenge: the impact of disruption. Disruption—questioning assumptions, taking risks, knowing that some attempts will fail, that there will be multiple iterations—was popular in those years especially in tech startups. I was not a fan of disruption per se, but it certainly turned out to be the way our process unfolded. We would make tremendous advances but also big mistakes. Like when we revised the schedule to make room for a new curriculum, which took time away from reading remediation, producing a dip in test scores. Or when the high school eliminated the demerit system, but without a plan to replace it, leading to a deterioration of student behavior. When a fight broke out inside one of our classrooms, I thought I would just fall apart. Seeing these struggles, a staffer at one of the foundations that had been supporting us concluded that our vision was unrealistic. "I appreciate what you're trying to do," she said. "I really do. Still, we can't wait a few years for results. And maybe it just can't be done in Harlem. Maybe you're making the perfect the enemy of the good."

But that was just it. For too long in public education, good had been considered good enough—for kids in low-income neighborhoods.[21]

I felt the weight of the world on my shoulders.

Larry knew this, as we spoke regularly. After one particularly difficult week, he emailed me. "I see what you are doing, no matter the challenges," he wrote. "Trust your instincts. Don't let anyone get in the way."

Around this time I came across a Beyoncé lyric: "If we're gonna heal, let it be glorious."[22] I copied it down and posted it on the wall by my desk as an inspirational reminder to stay the course. Sometimes, at the end of a hard day—another hard day—Kevin and I would tell each other, "It's going to be glorious!"

Others also kept the faith with me. Like Nathan Smith, our high school dean, a gentle, caring individual. "Without struggle, there is no progress," he would say, quoting Frederick Douglass. Nathan had joined us in our eighth year, just as our very first cohort of students had reached twelfth grade.[23] We had bonded over our shared commitment to teaching self-discipline, something that we talked about all the time, often while sitting on the roof after school. But we didn't have a system to implement our beliefs. We didn't know what an independence-based discipline system might look like.

Then, in 2015, we met Carol Lieber. Carol was an educator with over forty years of experience who had founded a secondary school in St. Louis in 1974, the same year Debbie Meier founded Central Park East. Carol had written books on school culture and discipline and, like Debbie and Dennis Littky, was an early member of Ted's coalition.[24] In the summer of 1966, she had lived in Chicago three blocks from Dr. King, and she'd attended many of his strategy meetings. "What I took away was King's indefatigable commitment to the role of listening and dialogue," she said. "King's work is the reason I became so committed to using restorative practices to anchor discipline." Carol called her approach "restorative accountable discipline."[25]

In the restorative process, if students break a rule, in addition to receiving a consequence, they are also required to take responsibility for their behavior—to repair the harm they've caused and restore their relationships within the school community, whether through a public or private apology or an act of kindness. Restorative discipline, Carol taught us, puts the onus on students to manage their behavior and character. This was the system that Nathan and I had been searching for.

Carol also taught us how to shift the way we interact with students when they do misbehave—to not lecture them but instead to seek to transform their attitude so they will be more likely to behave better in the future. "Carol taught me to stop preaching to the kids," Nathan said. "She told us, 'It's not about you. It's about the students taking responsibility for their behavior.' That really resonated, in zero time! I realized, *She's right, the kids are just tuning me out.* I thought, *I'm going to start tomorrow. I'm going to stop preaching.*"

Soon, Carol was a regular at our schools coaching our leadership team. It took two years for us to fully understand restorative discipline because she would not—could not—just give us quick fixes. She wanted to be sure that we were learning all the underlying theory and understanding every concrete detail. Ask one question, and you'd be sitting there an hour later trying to understand everything she told you in response. Carol was a walking encyclopedia.[26]

Another key part of our learning came from observing in private schools. We visited the Bank Street School, where Donna was sending her children; City and Country School, famous for its student jobs program; and the Masters School, which had been my inspiration for designing Harkness seminar rooms as the focal point of our high school.[27] We also spent time at our mentors' schools. BC and I visited Larry's High Tech High; Kevin and I went to see Ron's EL Polaris school; and several of us visited Shelley's Manhattan New School. At each, we could see and feel the values and vibe of its founder. In Ron's, the walls were filled with artwork that students had revised multiple times. In Shelley's, there were books everywhere, and bulletin boards were filled with student poetry alongside the poems of Robert Frost. In Larry's, the students were engrossed in interdisciplinary projects like building a bridge.

I realized that even as each school was unique in many ways, they all had something in common. It was their culture, which was intensely intellectual and meaningful. I recognized it; it felt like camp. More importantly, it was a stark contrast to the culture in so many schools—the commercially produced posters, the worksheets and PowerPoints, the corporate signage and sensibility. Somehow, the transmission of how schools should feel—meaningful and serious—had been lost in much of public education. This made our work feel all the more imperative.

Over time, more and more of our classrooms were beginning to reflect the kind of learning that I'd long hoped for. We were beginning to hit our stride.

Christine started with us as a third-grade math teacher in 2015. "In my old school," she said, "we had to follow a tightly controlled script that was sold to us new teachers as the best way to teach math. I still remember it. Step one: Demonstrate a procedure. Step two: Do it together. Step three: Drill over and over until memorized." Christine recalled the first time she visited our schools. "It felt like I had stepped into a private school. There was a warmth but also a seriousness about academics and a respect for students' abilities. In one of the classrooms I visited, students were debating two strategies to solve a math problem, and, at the same time, they were independently managing themselves, doing things like getting a ruler or protractor, then getting straight back to work. At my old school, we had to drill the students so they knew how to multiply using the standard algorithm. But at HVA, students understand *why* they are multiplying. They are taught to reason, debate, justify their arguments, have rationales for their thinking. They come to understand the purpose behind the math."

The spring of 2016 seemed like the right time to create a new faculty guide, a compendium of our educational philosophy and systems. Writing a new guide, I thought, would be important for codifying our ideas and protocols, because our vision was so different from what teachers were used to, so different from the norms in the schools where they used to teach. The first edition took about six months to draft and featured photos I had taken mostly at the private schools we'd visited, my hope being that presenting these models would clarify for our teachers what I believed about great teaching and why it mattered. As we had teachers analyze these models at our summer institute, they began to internalize the new ideas. They started to set up their classrooms and teaching structures to emulate the models. In subsequent editions of the guide, I was able to replace the private school photos with photos I took in our own classrooms. It was thrilling.

The new guide was more than a document. It was everything I believed and everything the team and I were trying to implement: intrinsic motivation, student agency, quality feedback, self-assessment, the value of notebooks over worksheets, restorative discipline, mindfulness, student ownership of the learning environment, student-led data analysis.

"I feel like the whole enterprise has reached a cosmic level," one of our first and most brilliant teachers said after reading the new guide. "This is groundbreaking and so, so necessary." Soon, the guide was circulating within the broader educational community, and other schools were using our ideas to elevate their work.

When a delegation of Harvard graduate students came to visit that year, one of them commented on the difficulty of implementing deeper learning in urban schools. "Over and over again," he said, "you're told it can't work. It can't actually happen in the classroom." But after spending the day at our schools, he'd seen that it was possible. "Seeing the classes in practice was pretty stunning," he said. "You see the teachers enact this deeper learning routine where you see them turn up the heat. You read the research—Magdalene Lampert writes about it, and Deborah Ball.[28] But I didn't believe this combination of systems and structures was possible. To see it in action is inspiring kind of beyond belief. I think that this place is really special. There's something to learn here that I don't know that you'll be able to see anywhere else."

Part II

4.

The Well-Educated Child

Any serious discussion about how to raise a well-educated child must begin by defining what it means to be well educated.

In my view, students who are well educated are intellectually curious, driven, and self-directed. They are interesting and interested. They recognize and appreciate beauty: the beauty of art, of music, the beauty of math. They are civil in discourse. Well-educated students are independent thinkers who are too savvy to be deceived. They can discern when governments are abusing power and can distinguish between credible information and propaganda. Their reaction when encountering new information is to assume that there's more to the issue in question. They are what Ted Sizer called "informed skeptics."

Skeptics, yes, but *informed* skeptics. In order for skepticism to be valuable, to be powerful, one first needs to know things. Thus, students must be knowledgeable and well read. James Baldwin spoke about reading Dostoyevsky, Nietzsche, Balzac, Richard Wright, Countee Cullen, Henry James. "I read everything," he said. "I read my way out of the two libraries in Harlem by the time I was thirteen."[1]

Students who are well educated are also kindhearted and attentive to the greater good, with a generous spirit, a wholesome character, and a strong moral sensibility.

Perhaps most importantly, being well educated means knowing how much you do not know. Humility is a sign of intelligence. A well-educated student has the good sense not to rush to judgment but first to study an issue before forming an opinion about it.

It follows, then, that one of a school's core responsibilities is to ensure that students read a substantial number of books: full books, books of lasting value. (This should be obvious, but alas it must be said.) Students should study great works of literature, political theory, oratory, autobiography, history, and philosophy. In his Nobel Prize lecture, Bob Dylan explained that his lyrics came from the "principles and sensibilities and informed view of the world" that he had gleaned from the books he'd read in school. "*Don Quixote, Ivanhoe, Robinson Crusoe, Gulliver's Travels, Tale of Two Cities,* all the rest—typical grammar school reading that gave you a way of looking at life, an understanding of human nature, and a standard to measure things by."[2]

School should be a place where the life of the mind is given ample room to develop. As such, schools must defend free inquiry, reject dogma, and privilege the unencumbered search for truth. School leaders must create a culture in which students are encouraged to express their views, are not beholden to what is popular, do not self-censor for fear of being shunned. We need to teach students how and why to engage in considered debate, and that arguing about ideas in good faith is how one sharpens one's mind. That it is important to examine the grounds of one's arguments, and to accede graciously, when appropriate, to stronger opinions.[3] That following the mob is neither cool nor sophisticated and is certainly not independent thinking.

School must also teach students to be good, decent people who treat one another with kindness and to do the right thing even when no one is watching.

Finally, while school must prepare students for college, career, and citizenship, its highest purpose is the shaping of the soul, the inner life. After all, if we convey to students that their entire K–12 experience is just preparation for something else, what kind of attitude will that engender as the years pass them by? We have these thirteen precious years to give students the chance to be fully present for their one and only childhood and adolescent education. To feel the thrill of insight that comes from working intensely with full intellectual engagement. To "be in awe," as Einstein said, "when contemplating the mysteries of eternity, of life, of the marvelous structures of reality."[4] To have exquisite learning experiences in which they become so absorbed that they enter a state of flow and do not even notice that they've been reading and working for hours.

A few months before Einstein died, a college student asked him if there was anything in which one could believe. "Try not to become a man of success," Einstein replied, "but rather try to become a man of value."

5.

Intellectual Aspirations

If you want to make sure that the children in your care are well educated, start by looking at the way their schools assess student learning.

Parents need to understand the outsized influence that assessment has within a school and what this means for the education their child is receiving. Assessment drives everything that happens in a school: curriculum, instruction, calendars, budgets, schedules, lesson plans, and ultimately *the entire educational experience of the child.* As a nation, if we do not get this right—and we have not—it will be impossible to get anything else about education right.

Sam Wineburg, founder of the Stanford History Education Group, explains that students can "crack multiple-choice questions using canny test-taking strategies" but will not do as well on assessments that ask them to justify their responses.[1] Especially significant are exit exams—those state tests that students must pass to graduate from high school, like the Regents in New York. If they are low quality, a curriculum that prepares students to pass them can undermine their readiness for college.

College readiness is about analytical thinking, research and writing, self-management, and persistence. It is, in short, about many of the qualities of a well-educated student that I described in chapter 4. As David Conley, the leading expert on college readiness,[2] explains, "Exit exams are problematic if they're directing teacher and student energy toward a type of learning that doesn't connect with college readiness. Those exams typically shy away from measuring or requiring anything that might be difficult to measure but is nevertheless important, such as a term paper, or a research project, or a lab-based experiment, or a critique of a source document."[3]

The inadequacy of state tests has long been understood by eminent educators. It has long been understood by private schools as well. Back when we opened our high school, I kept thinking about the fact that elite private schools in New York were exempt from the Regents. Those schools arguably offered the finest education available. If the Regents were not good enough for private schools, I thought, why should they be mandatory for our students in Harlem?

At first, I hoped that we could prepare our students for the Regents while also teaching "above" the test. But I eventually saw that our students were spending most of their time memorizing, while our talented teachers were constrained by the breadth—hence shallowness—of content that they had to plow through.[4] The exams were packed with so much information that the only way to prepare students was to speed through the curriculum, precluding any chance for reasoning, analysis, or the application of knowledge ("If a student drops his pencil, he misses a whole century of European history," Ted said[5]).

This is why so many private schools design their own curriculum and assessments. It's also why, in 1995, a group of prescient public school educators began to do the same, creating the New York Performance Standards Consortium, which received authorization to issue diplomas based on performance assessments, more complex and nuanced tests that measure students' ability to *apply* knowledge and skills.[6] I inquired about joining the consortium, but it was not taking new applications. I also met with a few members of the Board of Regents itself. They were sympathetic to our interest in a more ambitious curricular framework but confided that state policy was unlikely to change. Government bureaucracies move at a glacial pace.[7]

At one point, someone suggested that we move all the Regents Exams to middle school and have our high school students take AP tests. That sounded even worse to me, as it would have produced an inferior test-prep academic program in both middle *and* high school. I already had reason to be skeptical of the APs.

The year we started our high school, my younger daughter, Rachel, was taking AP Bio. Rachel had always loved science. She couldn't get enough of plants and animals, would read science books under her desk in history class, and had been intrigued by nature since kindergarten. But after enrolling in AP Bio, she said that she didn't like science class anymore. "What happened?" I asked. "It's boring," she said. "It's miserable. All we do is memorize."

That same year, the elite Scarsdale public schools eliminated the APs altogether in order to replace "mountains of memorization" with internally designed honors courses that culminate in extended research papers.[8] Their decision was intended to promote deeper learning. The principal of Scarsdale's high school wrote, "The AP curriculum does not mesh well with the intellectual aspirations we hold for our students. We are in the fortunate position to be able to deliver students richer courses of study in all disciplines that encourage higher-order thinking and habits of mind such as synthesis, evaluation, persistence, and tolerance for ambiguity in the face of difficult questions and problems."[9] Precisely. If it wasn't good enough for Scarsdale, it wasn't good enough for our students. I resolved that we would not be an AP school. We had more ambitious intellectual aspirations for our students as well.

This conviction, and the ensuing search for a more advanced academic framework, led to two of the most important decisions I'd make for our schools. The first was to delineate our own outcomes by creating a K–12 Graduate Profile: a statement of the competencies and traits that students should have by the time they graduate. In drafting the Graduate Profile, I organized the skills and attributes of a well-educated child into three domains: quality thinking, agency, and ethical purpose. These three domains, supported by the foundational ideas of free inquiry, humility, passion for knowledge, and appreciation for beauty, became our definition of deeper learning. Our plan was to backward-design our curriculum, instruction, and assessment from there.

The Graduate Profile was incomparably more meaningful and ambitious than the state graduation requirements.

Graduate Profile Summary

Graduate Profile

The Graduate Profile delineates the skills and attributes that students will develop over the course of their K-12 education.

QUALITY THINKING

Independent Thinking: I can discern the validity and accuracy of information.
Analysis: I can investigate and assess evidence to produce meaningful insights.
Problem Solving: I can use and evaluate multiple strategies to solve problems.
Communication: I can present information clearly and coherently, with precise language.
Persuasion: I can craft a compelling argument, supporting ideas with reliable evidence.
Innovation: I can develop original, creative, and groundbreaking ideas.
Intellectual Curiosity: I read avidly, and passionately pursue knowledge and understanding.

STUDENT AGENCY

Initiative: I can establish goals, design plans, and select strategies.
Responsibility: I can be accountable for my actions, preparation, punctuality, and organization.
Effort: I can work hard with energy, and put my best thinking into my work.
Focus: I can concentrate for long periods of time regardless of distractions.
Revision: I can use criteria, feedback, and reflection to revise and produce quality work.
Resourcefulness: I can figure out solutions, or get help when I am struggling.
Persistence: I can persevere through adversity to overcome obstacles and setbacks.

ETHICAL PURPOSE

Community: I can be a good friend, and help others to feel included.
Integrity: I can do the right thing regardless of what others do or whether anyone is watching.
Respect: I can value diverse opinions and be courteous with my words, actions, gestures, and tone.
Contribution: I can positively contribute to my class, grade, school, and community.
Loving Kindness: I can be caring, empathetic, and thoughtful to others.
Emotional Intelligence: I can recognize, understand, label, express, and regulate my emotions.
Social Justice: I can use my life in service of the greater good.

The second decision was to select the Montessori program for our PreK and the International Baccalaureate as our curricular framework in high school. Both aligned beautifully with our vision and, thus, with the outcomes in the Graduate Profile. The IB and Montessori both cultivate student agency, engage students in meaningful, challenging work that fosters intellectual curiosity, and require students to concentrate and persevere for extended periods of time on complex tasks.[10] In addition, the IB focuses on deep reading, academic discourse, research, and extended writing. I was attracted to the IB because of all this—and because of its use of performance assessment.

Performance assessment requires students to demonstrate their ability to transfer knowledge and skills to novel contexts. It measures the quality of student thinking and the depth of understanding through open-ended questions and complex tasks. As Ted said, the "real test for a student is when she is presented with something which is unfamiliar and asked to use what she has learned."[11] In science, for example, a performance assessment would require students to design, conduct, and analyze an original experiment: to formulate a hypothesis, select or develop reliable methods to test it, closely observe phenomena, interpret the resulting data, build models that explain it, write an original report, and complete an oral defense in front of experts.

IB assessments require both knowledge and the ability to apply knowledge as well as strong writing and oral presentation skills across all disciplines.[12] The IB literature exam, for instance, has students write several extended essays. The first requires them to reference multiple texts that they have covered in class in answering such questions as "In what ways are 'the contradictory' or 'the paradoxical' significant aspects of at least two of the works you have studied?" A second has them analyze a series of texts that have not been covered in class. Essays are graded on higher-order cognitive skills such as interpretation and analysis as well as on organization and focus. The oral exams ask students to analyze a literary text and a set of nonliterary texts through the lens of an important issue. Both the essays and the oral exams are evaluated by the world's most experienced IB teachers, selected and trained to ensure that the organization's global standards are applied consistently.

Imagine the brilliant teaching and learning necessary for students to be prepared to do well on such assessments.

With the Graduate Profile, we had reconceptualized the educational outcomes we wanted for our students. And with the IB, we had an infrastructure of exceptionally challenging assessment. The next step was to clarify the kind of teaching we would need to achieve our ambitious outcomes. We did this by creating our Deeper Learning Framework, a set of principles and practices for each of those three domains of deeper learning: quality thinking, agency, and ethical purpose. The next three chapters detail these in turn.

Part III

6.

Quality Thinking

The primary purpose of school, as Ted Sizer said, is to teach students to use their minds well.[1] This may seem obvious. After all, what is more fundamental to education than the intellectual development of students?

But, as Ted understood, the reality in most of our nation's schools is that students are not asked to think deeply or seriously or independently. Often, they are barely asked to think at all.

Consider one of the most common teaching methods: the presentation. In preparing for, say, a high school history class, a teacher will create a PowerPoint presentation by researching, evaluating, summarizing, and organizing information—all of which has the *teacher* engaged in higher-order thinking. In class, however, the students will take notes, a task that involves minimal cognitive demand.[2] We need to flip this. Instead of teachers presenting their best thinking, lessons should adeptly guide *students* to research, evaluate, summarize, organize, and present *their* best thinking.

Just as problematic as PowerPoints is the widespread use of fill-in-the-blank worksheets. "A friend of mine sent me a worksheet that was given to her child in middle school," Kevin said. "The questions were, number one, 'How important is math to you? Circle one.' There wasn't even a space to write. Then, 'What is your favorite number? Why?' and 'What's your favorite shape? Why?' How dare you insult a child with these questions! How dare you threaten our amazing profession with this nonsense."

Then there is the common teaching method known as "I do, we do, you do," typically used in American math instruction. Students watch the teacher, copy the teacher, then practice what they copied. To prepare such a lesson, a teacher will study, synthesize, and adapt complex material, often breaking it down into easier concepts. Again, high-cognitive-demand tasks for the teacher, oversimplified tasks for the students.

Another ubiquitous practice—one we all grew up with and most readily associate with school—is the raising of hands in response to a question: daily, hourly, constantly. While this may seem innocuous, it distracts from student thinking. Students often disengage once someone else is called on, rather than thinking themselves. Instead of a calm intellectual environment in which thoughtful questions are asked and all students are expected to think about them, attention is focused on the constant shooting up of hands. New teachers, mistaking raised hands for engagement, will encourage it ("I need to see more hands!"), while students, eager for participation points, will respond by raising hands to *appear* engaged.

The lowering of the intellectual bar has made its way into every aspect of academic life, even the language that is used in classrooms. New teachers are trained to use jargon like "attack a text" (read closely), "voices off" (be quiet), and "kiss your brain" (I don't even know what that one means). Children are now called "scholars," as if using this serious-sounding word conferred credibility on a school. Do we need to be reminded that a scholar is a seasoned academic with substantial expertise in a field of study? Why not refer to students as *children*, *class*, *friends*—or *students*, for crying out loud! This jargon is silly at best, pernicious at worst. The use of clear, precise language expands students' vocabulary and strengthens their command of linguistic nuance.

The quality of student thinking is further eroded by an overemphasis on test prep: repeatedly practicing techniques to answer questions on standardized exams. It isn't just that schools spend too much time preparing students for those exams (although they do) or that test prep narrows the curriculum and dominates the academic culture (although it does). It's that the academic disciplines themselves have devolved into a form of test prep. This was evident in a second-grade reading class I observed in the South Bronx. It was only October, long before the year-end state test, yet the entire lesson focused on test-prep questions about short, decontextualized passages ("Who can give me a solid answer statement that restates the question?"). It was evident when I asked a veteran principal from a highly respected school network for his thoughts on quality writing instruction, and he replied that he had not been trained in that.

He only knew the formula for writing answers to state test questions. And it was evident in a seventh-grade math lesson in another school where students were told that when they encounter a problem that is too difficult or taking too long, they should "just skip it—you can still get a good score with a few questions wrong." This is precisely the opposite of the persistence and intellectual struggle that students should be exercising in math.

Schools often function as if the students were not capable of handling cognitively demanding work. As Zaretta Hammond explains, "They struggle because we don't offer them sufficient opportunities in the classroom to develop the cognitive skills and habits of mind that would prepare them to take on more advanced academic tasks."[3] In other words, it's a self-fulfilling prophecy: If a school believes that students are unable to handle challenging classwork, it will teach in a way that does not challenge them, which means that they miss out on the chance to be challenged, which in turn produces students unable to handle challenging classwork.

"Almost every school that you visit will tell you that their goal is something around cognitive demand or higher-order thinking," said Peter, our math teacher who went on to be a lead architect of the New York State math curriculum. (He is now our math director.) "But then you look in the classrooms, and it's not happening—the tasks are not challenging; the instruction is procedural." A study by The Education Trust found that only 4 percent of class assignments "pushed student thinking to higher levels" and only 15 percent required students to do more than simply "recall information."[4]

The remedy for this intellectual malaise is to design academics to radically improve the quality of student thinking. We need to push students' thinking, elicit their best thinking, and teach them to think in a careful and deliberate manner.

In order to accomplish this, schools need an academic framework for quality thinking. And since quality thinking is so hard to execute well, schools should keep the framework simple. To this end, I offer five principles and four practices.

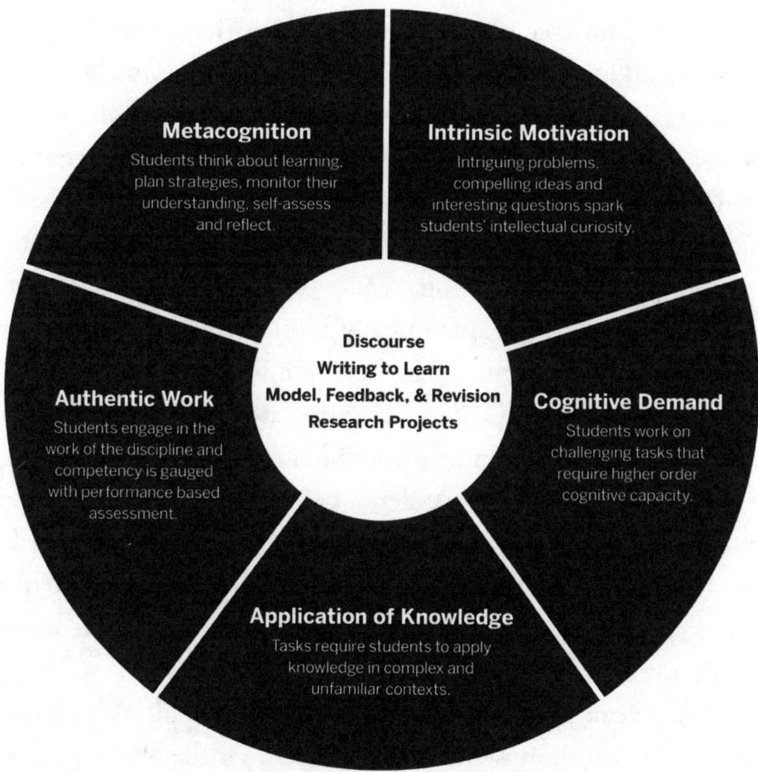

Quality Thinking: Principles & Practices

The first principle of quality thinking—intrinsic motivation—can be traced back to what we wrote in our founding charter application: "Imagine a school where students take their work home not because somebody told them that it's homework but because it's theirs, they're not done with it yet, the problem still needs solving, the question must be figured out." For learning to be intrinsically motivating, it must start with interesting questions, intriguing problems, and big ideas that spark intellectual curiosity.[5]

Intrinsic motivation is an inner drive that makes a person care about something because it holds value to them. As Dewey said, "An end which is the child's own carries him on to possess the means of its accomplishment."[6] When you *want* to understand something, you're driven from within to figure it out. When you want to accomplish something, you put in the work. You do it because you care.

When students are intrinsically motivated, they are driven not by reward or punishment but by interest, curiosity, intellectual fulfillment. Teachers can facilitate this inner drive. A teacher's role is not to motivate students but to create the conditions that will lead to students being self-motivated. These conditions, according to self-determination theory, are relatedness (feeling cared for and connected to others), competence (being productive and effective), and autonomy (having ownership over one's actions).[7]

Schools can foster relatedness by creating a culture of kindness and warmth in which students feel that they belong. This can be accomplished by beginning the school year with bonding experiences like camping trips, by spending time with students and really listening to them, by building close relationships with them based on trust and empathy, and by being involved in their lives in a way that shows them they are cared for. Schools can foster competence by engaging students in challenging work such as extended research projects that require them to compare and evaluate multiple original sources. And schools can foster autonomy by providing students with meaningful choices (for example, giving seventh graders the chance to decide which one of three short stories they will read), by offering the rationale for things they are asked to do in class or, better yet, eliciting the rationale (for example, asking a third-grade class, "Why do you think it's important to not laugh at each other when someone makes a mistake?"), and by providing clear direction and consistent structures.

Conversely, external incentives can stifle intrinsic motivation. Praise, punishment, and a focus on prizes or grades: These may produce short-term results but will ultimately foster apathy and diminish curiosity and initiative. When a school offers rewards or points for students to read, for example, they are likely to read shorter books or easier books or even pretend to read—anything to get the points. Intrinsic motivation can also be undermined by the misguided notion that engagement means entertainment, such as when schools encourage teachers to use songs or games to "make math fun." Instead, we should be designing lessons that cause students to be intrigued by *the math itself.*

When schools foster intrinsic motivation, students do not

need to be pushed to complete assignments. They are more focused and work harder and will push *themselves* to give their best effort.

In order to be intrinsically motivating, learning must be challenging—the second principle of quality thinking. One of the things we say all the time in our schools is that children are perfectly capable of work that is cognitively demanding. Zaretta often poses this question to drive home the point: When students are confused, how will we support them in a way that is *not* doing the work for them? The Russian psychologist Lev Vygotsky spoke of the zone of proximal development, the space that lies outside of, but adjacent to, a child's existing capabilities: the step that they're about to take—that they *could* take, with a little guidance. A challenging learning task places students in that zone.

At the most basic level, challenging our students requires giving them the chance to do the work in the first place. As Bob Moses, the founder of the Algebra Project, explained, students should be less like spectators and more like players doing the work of the "sport," with teachers as coaches.[8] This idea was intended to address the widespread problem of teachers doing more of the intellectual work than students. Whoever is doing most of the reading, writing, speaking, and creating in a classroom—the teacher or the student—is the one who is doing the thinking. (In our charter application, we called this "students doing the intellectual heavy lifting.")

Then it is a matter of making sure that the task, the text, and the questions are appropriately difficult—pushing students to struggle intellectually, to think beyond the conventional, beyond common assumptions. When Christine was teaching fourth-grade math, she was responsible for the following state standard: "Compare two fractions with different numerators and different denominators (for instance, 3/4 and 2/3) by creating common denominators or numerators, or by comparing to a benchmark fraction such as 1/2. Recognize that comparisons are valid only when the two fractions refer to the same whole." She started her lesson, as we have taught our math teachers to do, with a problem. "I wrote a simple equation on the board, 10 = 10," she said, "and I asked, 'Does ten equal ten?' And they all said, 'Yeah, ten equals ten.' Then I asked, 'Does two equal two?' and they said, 'Yes.' And, 'Does one equal one?' Again, 'Yes.' Then I asked, 'So does one large pizza equal one small pizza?' And they said, 'No.' I said, 'But you said one equals one. Can you prove that one does not always equal one?' And they were just, like, minds blown.

"I asked them to draw models using their individual whiteboards. Then they had all kinds of arguments. Most of the kids were now saying, 'One does not always equal one because one big pizza doesn't equal one small pizza.' Some kids were trying to explain that they have to be the same size. But other kids were confused. It became this back-and-forth. And one student, Faith, she was like, 'I understand what you're saying, but it doesn't make sense that one is not the same as one. We know one penny is one penny.' Then another student said, 'But when you get a soda, you get a small or a large, and they are not equal.'

"I had the whole class working to convince each other of whatever they were thinking. Some were changing others' minds. See, they can compare two fractions just by looking at the numerator if the denominator is the same, but only if the whole is the same size. They're taught it's really easy—like, procedurally, here's how to compare. But now they were learning that isn't always the case. The sizes of the wholes are different, so the quantity is different. I asked them to prove their thinking. At one point, another student said to Faith, 'If half is half, would you rather have half of a poor person's money or half of a rich person's money?' And that's when she had an 'aha' moment, and she finally agreed that one is not always one.

"The ultimate goal of this lesson was to take what they had already learned and kind of blow it up a little bit, so that they would realize that math is not just about rules. You have to defend your thinking, articulate your thinking. Do you agree or disagree? What do you believe to be true?"

The determination to challenge students can fall apart when schools encounter students who struggle academically. All too often the response is to lower standards, ostensibly out of empathy for the child. But if schools believe, as we do, that lowering standards is not in a child's best interest, we need to figure out how to help students who are struggling so they can meet the high bar of challenging work.

Lucas is a quirky and sweet third grader with a learning disability. He has a hearing impairment and, as a result, he missed out on a lot of the oral language development that happens from birth to kindergarten. "It's hard to know exactly what he's hearing and not hearing," Kevin said. "So he's not starting at the starting line; he's forty miles back." This is a kid who touches everyone's heart. But academically, he is struggling with our high standards.

Kevin, who is Lucas's principal, took it upon himself to tutor him personally. In fact, *principal* comes from the Latin *principalis*, or "first." The word originated in the idea that the school leader is the first or foremost teacher in the school.[9] Kevin is the quintessential principal teacher. He tutors many struggling children after school and on Saturdays.

"I've been working with Lucas nonstop. He struggles and struggles and struggles," Kevin said. "We've been studying fractions. Every step of the way is lumbered and labored for him. He has trouble expressing what he wants to say."

One of our core ideas from our first year has been "keeping pace rather than catching up." This means that we provide small-group instruction and tutoring, sometimes daily, for students who need extra help (whom we identify through baseline assessments before the start of the school year), so they can keep up with the challenging learning in class each day. This is far more effective than waiting for them to fail and then trying to remediate at the end of the week (or worse, at the end of the unit of study, when the class has moved on to other topics). This system is imperative because in any given class there will always be a wide range of abilities. Some students will be ready for accelerated work (which we provide); some will be doing fine, learning the material within the allotted class time; some will need extra support occasionally or for a specific issue; and some will need extra time and support throughout the year.

Lucas was in the last category, so he was placed in a small tutoring group that met for several sessions during the week plus an extra one on Saturdays to reinforce the week's lessons. In one session, the lesson focused on how to build fractions that are equal to other fractions.[10] The first thing Kevin did was ask the children to build fractions using fraction strips (small strips of plastic that are proportionally the size of each fraction and have the corresponding fraction written on them). He told the children to use them to find as many fractions as they could that were equal to one-half. Lucas was able to do this: He was able to take two quarter-length strips and put them together to make a half, and he was able to take four eighths and do the same.

Then Kevin told the children to write those fractions out. Lucas wrote, "2/4, 3/6, 4/8." So far, so good. But then he wrote, "2/3." "When I saw that," Kevin said, "I knew he wasn't grasping the concept that the numerator and denominator need to have a one-to-two relationship. Most of the other kids got it, but he didn't." Lucas was looking for patterns, which is good. But because one is one less than two, his confusion was in thinking that the numerator just needs to be one less than the denominator—a common misconception for third graders.

So Kevin had Lucas go back to the beginning and work through it again. He said, "Lucas, go to the fraction strips again and make fractions that equal one-half." After Lucas had done that, Kevin asked, "Lucas, look at what you've built.

What do you notice about the fractions?" Lucas said he noticed that you could line them up so they are even. "That was a glimmer of hope," Kevin said. Next Kevin asked, "Can you draw these fractions in your math notebook? Draw a picture of what you built." Lucas did that as well. He was starting to understand. Kevin asked him what else he noticed, but he couldn't yet articulate the concept of equivalent fractions. So Kevin offered this: "Could you say they're the same size?" And that's when the light bulb went on. "Yes!" Lucas said. "So what's something that is true about equivalent fractions?" Kevin asked. "They are the same size," Lucas said. He was starting to understand that equivalent fractions are fractions that are the same size.

"He can get there," Kevin said. "He just doesn't get there as fast as the other kids."

And that's the beauty part. In a school where not all students are challenged, Lucas would have simply earned a C-minus or D, and the class would have moved on without him. What's worse, he would have missed out on mastering a skill that is a prerequisite for learning the skills that will be taught next. When the time invested in each student is fixed, student achievement becomes variable. We must reverse this. Time and support should be flexible based on each student's needs. What must be fixed is our belief that all students are capable of handling cognitively demanding work.[11]

One way to keep students appropriately challenged is to make sure they are doing work that is authentic. This is the third principle of quality thinking: Students should do the authentic work of each discipline they study, the work that is done by adult practitioners. In writing, this means students do what writers do: read avidly to internalize the fundamentals of quality writing, organize and outline their ideas, and continually revise. In history, it means evaluating sources for validity, making sense of conflicting accounts, and seeking to understand why a given question matters in the first place. In science, it means designing and conducting experiments in a laboratory setting, or, as we saw students doing when we visited High Tech High, building rockets and robots. In math, it means grappling with problems and proofs, designing new theories, and evaluating various strategies to solve problems. As Jerome Bruner said, "Being able to go beyond the information given to figure things out is one of the few untarnishable joys of life." And more than joy, Bruner explained that when students figure things out on their own, they are "rearranging or transforming evidence in such a way that one is enabled to go beyond the evidence" to "new insights."[12] *This* is what we want for students: to experience the thrill and discipline required to produce insights from engaging in authentic work.

The fourth principle of quality thinking is application of knowledge, also known as transfer. In order to think deeply, students need to be able to apply or transfer the knowledge and skills that they acquire in one context to different and unfamiliar contexts.

Grant said that transfer is arguably the entire purpose of

education.[13] And the influential "Teach for Understanding" research project came to define *understanding* itself as "the ability and inclination to use what one knows."[14] As explained in *How People Learn*, the definitive work on learning theory, students in a typical science class "may be expected to remember that arteries are thicker than veins, are more elastic, and carry blood from the heart," but the application of that knowledge would require them to "understand *why* veins and arteries have particular properties" so as to be equipped, for example, to design an artificial artery.[15] The promise of deeper learning is the promise of students who are capable of such ingenious, agile thinking—the kind of thinking that can prepare the next generation of scientists to summon insights that could prevent pandemics, or entrepreneurs to come up with innovative ideas, or the next environmental scientists to avert climate disaster.

The fifth and final principle of quality thinking is metacognition, the practice of monitoring and directing one's thinking.[16] Metacognition is a recursive cycle of investigation, inference, hypothesis, and reflection. It starts with a question, problem, task, or goal. It continues as students begin working while self-monitoring their understanding, allocating their time, and figuring out how to overcome obstacles. Then they continue to revise their thinking as they get new information. The cycle culminates in reflection. This last phase is critical. John Hattie explains that reflection is not simply "looking back"; it is a "disciplined way of thinking."[17] That is, the very process of reflecting on how one's thinking has developed is what deepens one's thinking.

Take our protocol for error analysis. After students take a math test, teachers hand the tests back with incorrect answers circled. Students review their mistakes and, sometimes working in pairs, ask themselves: What misunderstandings do my errors reveal?

In the IB curriculum, students' metacognitive capacity is strengthened through the study of epistemology. Every student takes the IB Theory of Knowledge course, where they ask the question "How do I know what I know?" They contemplate the nature, scope, and limitations of knowledge. They consider "contestable questions about knowledge itself—Are some types of knowledge less open to interpretation than others?" and "How is knowledge arrived at in different disciplines?"[18]

"Metacognition is the cognitive foundation of all of the work students do," BC said. When BC was mentoring our middle school science and social studies teachers, she designed a unit on earthquakes for fifth graders. It started with each class learning about a court case in Italy in which residents in the medieval town of L'Aquila had reported small and medium tremors for months. A national commission had convened a panel of seismologists and geologists who met but did not issue any warning. A week later, on April 6, 2009, a 6.3-magnitude earthquake killed 309 people. The scientists were put on trial for negligent homicide and convicted of providing false reassurances to citizens, but the American Association for the Advancement of Science condemned the verdict.[19]

Students were asked: Was it fair and reasonable to accuse these scientists? This led to one of the big essential questions of the unit: Can scientists predict where and when earthquakes will happen, and if so, to what degree of certainty? "We asked students what we would need to know to address this question," BC said. "We had them look at continental shelf maps and contour maps of where earthquakes were common so they could understand the patterns of earthquakes. We had different groups looking at different high earthquake zones—Indonesia, Japan, California—to find similarities based on the maps and, through deductive reasoning, to draw some preliminary conclusions about what kinds of areas are most likely to produce an earthquake. Most of the students deduced that earthquakes happen in places with rocky mountains where continental shelves come together. Although the pattern is around 90 percent, it's not perfect. One student noticed that. While other kids were focusing on the patterns, he said, with all this enthusiasm, 'But look at the outliers!' It was a perfect moment. He was totally interested in these couple of atypical examples." This kind of intellectual engagement would not have happened if the students had simply sat to take notes on a lecture about earthquakes.

The next lessons continued the metacognitive process. "We showed students images and videos of an earthquake," BC continued. "They studied three basic kinds of aftereffects, and we had them create scientific drawings in their notebooks of what is going on under the ground to produce them." Then students worked in small groups. "We blew up a large graphic of the layers of rock in the earth. Students discussed the explanations for what's happening above and below the ground. They were thinking and arguing about what's happening before and during and after the earthquake. Based on this, they revised their images, and this time included annotations to show forces and describe the two pieces of a continental shelf coming together. We then did a number of experiments where students worked with rocks and seismographs to see how different movements of the rocks affected the seismograph. They revised their images again, and each time came to a clearer and clearer articulation of the forces underneath the ground." This is metacognition: Learners are continually refining, expanding, and deepening their thinking based on new information.

"The purpose of studying earthquakes in middle school earth science," BC said, "is for students to understand the layers of the earth, that what is beneath the earth is constantly changing, and that earthquakes are created by forces and pressure. Understanding the nature of that pressure is an introduction to the idea of forces and waves in physics." BC had used Grant's *Understanding by Design* approach, designing curriculum around big concepts and starting with a meaningful question. "We open with why the topic matters," she said. "There are essential questions for each group of lessons in the unit. What causes earthquakes and what happens when earthquakes happen? How can a rock bend, how can earth move? How do scientists use models to help understand things?"

For their final project, the students had to use what they learned to design a house that is earthquake-proof. "They had to make sure the structure could maintain its integrity," BC said. With their understanding now sufficiently deep and detailed, they could approach this challenging task with confidence.

The five principles of quality thinking—intrinsic motivation, cognitive demand, authentic work, application of knowledge, and metacognition—are derived from decades of scholarship in the field of learning science. And while there are many ways to implement those principles in the classroom, we have determined that four core practices offer the greatest leverage for promoting quality student thinking. They also have the virtue of being relevant to virtually all subjects and grade levels.

The first core practice for quality thinking is discourse: structured academic discussion in which students are reasoning, questioning, and interpreting. Discourse can take many forms, including teacher-led discussions, small group or partner talk, and Socratic seminar.

One of the most compelling frameworks for discourse in the classroom is Lauren Resnick's concept of accountable talk, with its "three accountabilities": "accountability to knowledge (getting the facts right)," "accountability to reasoning (providing a rational justification for a claim)," and "accountability to community (showing respect for . . . classmates)."[20] For discourse to be effective, teachers need to hold students to a high standard of accuracy, ensuring that they "work hard at 'getting it right': Are those statistics accurate? Where did they come from? What is your basis for that conclusion? Who said that?"

Teachers also need to insist on a high standard for student reasoning. "Making cogent and compelling arguments requires linking together claims and evidence in a logical, coherent, and rigorous manner."[21] And teachers need to teach students how to interact respectfully.

There is a misperception that discourse ought to be completely student led. Not so. The teacher's role is essential. The teacher needs to orchestrate quality discourse by listening carefully, pushing students to offer their most incisive commentary possible, and intervening when needed to get students back on track. As Resnick explains, it should be a "*teacher-led* but *student-owned* process of shared reasoning that ultimately leads to a more fully developed, evidence-backed conclusion, solution, or explanation."[22]

One form of discourse, the Socratic seminar, has long been a cornerstone of elite education. (When we designed our high school building, we built three seminar rooms for this purpose.) Teachers prepare for seminar by thoughtfully planning readings, protocols, methods for evaluation, and open-ended questions to which there is no one simple or right answer. Students prepare by reading great works of literature or other complex texts, annotating the texts, and formulating their arguments with care. During seminar, texts are open on desks, and students are expected to cite them directly in support of their arguments as they debate the questions.

In studying *The Catcher in the Rye*, for instance, "students will read and annotate studies of Salinger's life," our IB director, David Quinn, explains, "to examine the reaction to the novel at the time it was written. Then they will read and discuss historical and biographical information—for example, the impact of World War II on social norms and how it may have affected the author. They then return to the original text to analyze how those norms play out in the novel."

Another method we use to elevate the quality of student discourse is a protocol we've named "Ask all, then call," which we designed to address the perpetual problem of students disengaging once another student is called on. When a teacher poses a question to the whole class, students do not raise their hands in response. (This takes some getting used to.) Instead, they are all expected to be thinking. Only after a few moments does the teacher call on someone. But this is not simply a cold-call technique. The point is to make sure that all students are thinking throughout the lesson about every question so as to build the habit of genuinely engaging their minds.

Just as discourse requires and develops thinking, so too does writing. Thus, the second core practice to foster quality thinking is the use of "writing to learn" in all disciplines. This is different from learning to write well in English class. It is writing as a tool for learning in any subject, as the process of articulating one's ideas in writing serves to sharpen one's thinking.[23] That is why for years I have pushed for the use of notebooks, which we now incorporate in virtually all subjects and grades across our schools. Even something as simple as setting up a new page, with the date and learning target, at the beginning of each lesson teaches students to create systems to organize information. Whereas with worksheets (still the coin of the realm in many classrooms), the teacher does the organizing for them.

At the beginning of our math lessons, to take one example of how we use writing to learn, the teacher poses a problem, then students try to work it out in their notebooks. They almost always make mistakes, especially on the first try. "If there are no mistakes," Peter says, "you're not doing it right; it's not problem-based math." As students wrestle with the problem, the teacher walks around the classroom, looking at their work and strategically selecting examples that are correct, partially correct, or even incorrect that can be used to highlight common misconceptions or push student thinking. The teacher then displays that work with the document camera and leads the class in a discussion of what they've just done. Sometimes students will be called up to the board to explain how they approached the problem. All the while, the class is revising their mathematical models or otherwise modifying their own work in their notebooks.

The teacher will then pose a new problem, and students will try again, also in their notebooks. After several cycles of problem-solving, practice, and discourse, students synthesize their thinking by writing a summary of what they have learned, which helps them to reinforce their understanding of the lesson's learning target. Students may also write to keep track of their thinking as their understanding develops over the course of the week or a unit. It is often while reviewing what they have written that they come to "aha" moments of insight.

Using notebooks in this way requires and promotes agency and metacognition.

Even young students are perfectly capable of doing all this if we give them the opportunity. A class of third graders, for example, recently wrote math reflections, something we have students do periodically. "I struggled in math," Ethan wrote. "I felt sad and mad. I was not thinking about the question before I answered it. Now I read the question two times." Luna wrote: "I felt frustrated about math. To improve I tried asking for help, working hard during the weekend with my homework and asking for help when I needed it, and I am reading the question three times. To keep getting better I can keep doing these things. Currently I feel happy about math." Another student, Noah, had a more practical realization: "I felt that I was not ready for third grade. I struggled in finishing my work in math. To improve, I had to do my work instead of talking to the kids next to me." And Sophia wrote, "I felt mad about math because it was a little bit hard for me. I push through and try my best. To keep getting better I ask for help when I need it, and I do more than one strategy. Now math makes me happy even if it is hard."

Similarly, in independent reading, we set aside time each month for students to self-assess their growth as readers and to write about the ways they want to improve their reading habits. We provide special notebooks where students self-manage their reading, keep a list of what books they have read, maintain a list of books they might want to read next, and, most importantly, write about themselves as readers. This encourages them to take seriously the idea of cultivating a reading life, as opposed to the typical approach of using a reading log or worksheet that parents sign as a compliance tool but that kids can easily game by filling in page numbers without actually having read anything. (I remember doing this myself in school!) And because they have the experience of doing what avid readers do (choosing books, reflecting on what they have read, getting lost in a good book, thinking about what they want to read next), they become avid readers.

"I feel that I've grown as a reader because I am now willing to read more variety," wrote Chloe, an eighth grader. "I have an openness to being exposed to different types of books. In January, I finished five books: *And We Rise*, *My Name Is Jason. Mine Too.*, *The Black Kids*, *50 Fearless Women Who Made American History*, and *Macbeth*. I feel empowered that I can choose any of the books in the library, even really challenging ones like Shakespeare." Joseph, also in eighth grade, wrote, "Last month, I tried pushing myself to read more nonfiction books and I feel I've succeeded in that regard. This month, if there's a book I might be interested in, I'll try it. Last month my goal was to read three books. This month, my goal will be to read four books." Liam, a sixth grader, wrote, "I've realized that I love reading about the past. I get in the zone when I'm reading about history." And eighth grader Olivia wrote, "I read *The Three Theban Plays* by Sophocles. I strongly believe I should keep reading as I got into a good rhythm of reading at school and home. I will explore another genre next month."

Having students take responsibility for their learning in this way causes them to care about their learning, which is transformative.

The third core practice for quality student thinking is the cycle of model, feedback, and revision. Studying and emulating models of great work is a long-standing way of learning. Ron first talked with us about model-feedback-revision when he was training our leaders. He told us the story of a high school physics teacher who spent years trying to get her students to write good lab reports. She had tried to improve her rubrics, refining criteria like "introduction provides a clear summary" and "data is well organized," but to no avail. Ron suggested that she find an exemplary lab report and share it with her students. As soon as they received it, she could see the light bulbs go on. Their lab reports improved considerably. When you give students a list or rubric with abstract criteria, some of them will understand some of the criteria, but many will misunderstand or not understand at all. But show them a concrete model and ask them to determine what makes it good, and most students will understand.

The protocol Ron taught us, which we now use regularly to great effect, begins with the teacher presenting a model—a history paper, a scientific graph, an argumentative essay—for students to examine. They study it closely to discern the attributes that make it exemplary, then write down everything they notice (they can also brainstorm in pairs). Then the class discusses their observations as the teacher writes them on chart paper, refining for accuracy and rephrasing for clarity. These become the criteria for the task at hand, and, having derived them by observing and analyzing carefully, the students now understand what they're working toward. They are ready to create their own first drafts.

At this point, the cycle of feedback and revision begins. Students use feedback—from the teacher and from peers (who are also steeped in the criteria)—to continually revise their drafts. They also revise based on their own self-assessment. The idea is to instill the habit of revision. And so it goes, through an iterative process of reflecting on feedback, revising, referring to the model or criteria, reworking, repolishing, then asking for more feedback. Once a final version is completed, student work is displayed on bulletin boards, ideally featuring all the versions to highlight the value of revision.

Grant wrote that "feedback is among the most powerful influences on achievement," but he also said that much of the feedback he observed was ineffectual. So he formulated guidelines: Feedback must be clear, timely, understandable, actionable, and made in reference to a goal.[24] Ron's criteria were that feedback should be kind, specific, and helpful.

Feedback, done well, is not just giving students notes but teaching them "to receive, interpret, and use that feedback."[25] In our charter application, we had written that feedback "should cause students to want to keep working." In other words, we wanted students to become intrinsically motivated to care about the quality of their work as well as proficient in using feedback to improve—capable of understanding how feedback illuminates gaps between their draft and the model and, as with peer critique in graduate school, capable of generating useful feedback themselves.

The first three practices—discourse, writing to learn, and model-feedback-revision—can take place in every grade throughout the day, usually embedded within lessons. Teachers can have students engage in academic discourse or analyze a model or write in their notebooks during class in any subject. But students also need the opportunity to extensively research and intensively study one topic so deeply that they come to know what it means to truly understand something. In so doing, they learn to be skeptical when encountering any form of information. This is why the final core practice for quality thinking—the research project—is so critical to a complete education. This *single* practice fosters virtually *all* the higher-order cognitive skills and agency skills in our Graduate Profile.

Research projects are usually conducted over the course of several months, often an entire year. Students choose a topic worthy of inquiry, design a quality research question, engage with a range of facts and opinions, determine the reliability of multiple sources, organize information, summarize and synthesize, seek advice, and revise their work. Teachers do not mark up students' papers; they provide feedback, but students must take responsibility for the actual revisions. Then students are expected to present their findings and conclusions in a reasoned and coherent manner. And they need to do this multiple times and with increasing levels of complexity as they progress from elementary through high school. This experience is profound because studying one topic in-depth for an extended period of time confers a critical perspective on all *other* information students will encounter. They learn what it takes to prove something, to establish it with any degree of certainty, and how difficult it is to really be sure about information.

These and other deeper learning practices can produce breathtaking results. And this is what the principles and practices of quality thinking can create in every school: a vibrant academic culture where students are struggling with complexity, concentrating for long stretches of uninterrupted time on challenging tasks, enthralled with reading and with knowledge, and obsessed with revision and quality work.

7.

Agency

Students cannot learn to think independently in schools that do not allow them to act and work independently—that is, to exercise agency.

Agency is the capacity to be self-directed. Students with agency take initiative and push through difficulties, going beyond what is required. They are self-motivated: on fire to achieve their goals, read more books, pursue more challenging work.

Agency is one of the most consequential components of a world-class education. That is why it has been an enduring idea in educational thinking, the subject of a vast body of scholarship.[1] College readiness itself depends on agency, on "the degree to which students take ownership of their learning and are allowed to do so."[2]

Yet the defining feature of urban schooling is the antithesis of agency: extremely tight management of students. New teachers are trained to micromanage students with techniques like snapping, clapping, chanting, doling out verbal rewards for correct answers ("bonus!"), and using color-coded charts to keep track of student behavior. There is incessant praise for basic actions ("I like how Sam is silently waiting. I like how Britney is silently waiting. I like how Rodney is silently waiting."). There is rapid, staccato narration ("Your thinking job is character motivation. What's your thinking job? Track Caylee! Rudy's hands are locked tracking Caylee! Elijah's hands are locked tracking Caylee! Glory's hands are locked tracking Caylee!" Finally, Caylee answers: "Character motivation." The teacher says, "Nice job, Caylee!" The class repeats, "Nice job, Caylee!"). Schools use classroom rugs with predesignated squares to prescribe exactly where each student should sit and tactics like "magic five" to prescribe exactly how they should sit (rigidly upright in pin-straight rows, hands clasped or "locked" at all times). Teachers are told to control their students' every move, counting down after each direction ("Trade papers with your partner in ten, nine, eight, seven, six, five, four, and three, and two, one, and zero"). Jumbo timers are the focal point of the classroom, beeping throughout the lesson. Students hear these inane directives, countdowns, and beepers in class after class, day after day—stifling their independence at every turn and sending the message, clear as can be, that they are incapable of managing even the simplest tasks.

Martin Haberman exposed this excessive micromanagement of students, calling it the "pedagogy of poverty."[3] These methods have become so common that they are not even recognized as inferior but simply accepted as normal, even great teaching.

This is not great teaching. It reduces learning to rote repetition, impedes critical and logical thinking, undermines emotional intelligence, and shapes young minds to value conformity and compliance. It is incongruous with a century of scholarship on learning theory and cognitive science.

Which is why these methods are not found—and would not be tolerated—in our nation's finest private and suburban schools, where students are educated with a very different approach based on very different assumptions about what children are capable of and what great teaching is.

Consider, for example, the independence and Emersonian self-reliance that children learn in Montessori schools, over 90 percent of which are private. In the Montessori method, "the children navigate the classroom independently with minimal teacher direction," says Melissa Ortiz, our Montessori early learning director who was one of our founding kindergarten teachers. "The Montessori teacher serves as an adept guide. After introducing students to a new lesson, the teacher carefully observes to determine what each student understands. The whole idea is for the teacher to build independence and mastery concurrently."

The Montessori method was founded on the primacy of agency. Maria Montessori wrote that her method was designed to encourage in children "a burst of independence of all unnecessary assistance that suppresses their activity and prevents them from demonstrating their own capacities. These children reveal to us the most vital need of their development, saying: Help me to do it alone!"[4]

Agency is also central to the International Baccalaureate, which designed its entire approach "to empower students to become self-regulated learners."[5] Students educated in this way—with agency as a core pedagogical value—learn to be self-starters who seek out knowledge, sustain focus, monitor their own progress, and persist through setbacks.

The development of agency requires a shift in school culture as well as an infrastructure of classroom practices that can teach the skills of self-direction. Routines, for example, are procedures for how to go about each aspect of the school day—how to participate appropriately in a class discussion, turn in homework, organize course materials, walk in the hallway, and so forth.

Our original routines were designed to foster kindness and respect. Each year a new cohort of fifth graders arrived from other schools that tolerated poor behaviors, which then developed into habits: fidgeting, shuffling, tapping, humming, mumbling, slouching, facing sideways, playing with belongings, clicking binders, and in some cases teasing, cursing, refusing to work, or disrupting lessons. Back then it was a real problem.

But not for Rebecca. She made sure that her students were listening, looking, and respectfully focused on the lesson. She created routines for every learning activity, explained what was expected ("We're about to file our papers into our binders, and here's how it will work . . ."), then had students practice them.

I was fascinated by the engagement and behavior she

produced, so I planted myself in the back of her classroom for a few days to study what she was doing and started to read up on the psychology of habits. Rebecca's demeanor was calm and very soft, but she was deliberate, firm, and unrelenting in her insistence that every single student meet every expectation in every lesson. "Kareem, sit up. Victoria, eyes on me. Damon, listen to Victoria. Stephan, you've *got* to have your eyes on me so I know you are listening." She set the bar high and they met it. "Brandon, sit up straight," she said at one point. And when he responded by sitting up halfway, she fixed her gaze on him and said, softly but in a tone that conveyed she meant business, "*Really* straight." By Thanksgiving, she no longer needed to insist or even remind her students of her expectations. They had gotten so much practice that the positive behaviors had become their new habits. More importantly, by insisting on excellence from 100 percent of her students, she was sending a tacit message that every child was capable, and every child mattered.

The best way to unlearn old habits is to "replace not erase"—to start a new behavior rather than just trying to stop the old one. It takes about seven weeks of constant practice for new behaviors to turn into habits. "When a new habit is practiced through countless repetitions," writes Daniel Goleman, "the neural circuitry becomes the brain's default option."[6]

We developed a three-day student orientation for the beginning of each school year. It consisted of a series of lessons to teach and practice routines so they would become habits. To create these lessons, I led teachers through a design exercise.

"Close your eyes and visualize your ideal classroom," I said. "How are students behaving? What does it look and sound like, what does it feel like?" I asked them to write about what they had visualized, then had them share ideas and collaborate on plans.

"I want the kids to listen respectfully," one teacher said. "That was in my visualization also, *really* listening," said another. In fact, every teacher had some version of students focused, looking and listening throughout class. "In my visualization, the kids are laughing at my jokes, but then they are able to get back to work quickly," said a third teacher. This became a routine we created to "bring it back" so teachers could move seamlessly from jovial moments back to learning. We taught kids that there will be times when they need to transition from loud to silent work, so if they hear the teacher say "bring it back," that means they need to immediately be silent and look at the teacher. Then we made a fun game of practicing this a few times so they would get the hang of it. And we provided the rationale that if they can do this quickly every time, it will save a lot of learning time *and* prevent boredom.

"Are we going to allow sharpening pencils in the middle of a lesson?" someone asked. "That drives me crazy. The kid goes to the pencil sharpener and then comes back, and I have to repeat what I just said, which is boring for the rest of the class." Everyone agreed: There should be no getting up to sharpen pencils in the middle of a lesson. "And if they show up to class without their pencils, that's a demerit. Problem solved!" one teacher said. "Wait—hold on," another replied. "I want to teach, not give out demerits all day to kids who need a pencil." I had been talking about preventive discipline since the day we opened. "The whole point," I said now, "is to prevent the problem in the first place, not punish it after." That's when the group came up with the idea of having students sharpen six pencils at home each night so they would come to school prepared the next morning.

These were the kinds of details that went into designing classroom management routines to ensure good behavior and optimize learning time. The pencil discussion was one of many. We created routines for homework folders, notebooks, lunch and recess, arrival and dismissal, entering and exiting the classroom, disagreeing respectfully, being courteous in the hallway. We crafted explicit plans for every detail of every desired behavior, and we taught the rationale for every routine so we could inspire the students to care about being respectful. Something as simple as arrival, for instance, is an opportunity to teach courtesy. We teach students to look behind them when they enter the building so they can hold the door open if someone is entering after them, and we teach them to greet the security guard with kindness and respect rather than just passing by. The expectation of timely arrival is also an opportunity to teach responsibility and time management. We give students a detailed "backward planning" lesson that starts with figuring out what time they need to go to bed in order to get enough sleep, and what time they will get their materials organized in the evening so they will not forget something in the morning rush. Then they map out how long it will take to commute or walk to school (they have to add time to account for inevitable delays), then how long it will take to get dressed, all the way back to when they need to wake up.

We created fifteen lessons altogether, and to make them fun, the teachers created skits and songs and even some practical jokes. We also created associated classwork and posters. During orientation and the first weeks of school, teachers observed one another's classrooms, then after school each day we analyzed the efficacy of each routine, learned from our mistakes, solved problems, and made adjustments for the next day—like when we planned for all students to transition between classes at the same time but neglected to think about how it would work and discovered that kids were walking into one another! We spent that night drawing out hallway-transition maps. Or when we realized that our "bring it back" protocol would not work well if kids were talking loudly, as that meant the teacher would have to yell over them to be heard, thus setting a bad example, so we adjusted to a more effective call for silence in those situations—a single hand in the air—which became our signal for students to immediately stop and silently look at the teacher.

All this—our high expectations, our strict rules and loving culture, our drive to continually improve and to insist on excellence—produced an amazing school culture. You could walk into almost any classroom and see an entire class of kids who were attentive, genuinely happy, behaving well, and intellectually engaged. It was a joy.

•

But there was a problem with our approach, though we didn't realize it at the time. The adults were doing all the work. The adults were designing classroom management plans, telling students how to follow them, evaluating students, coming up with ideas to solve problems when they arose, revising plans, and pushing for excellence. Because they had ownership of all this work, the adults were committed and energized; the students were just following along.

That was the first thing that our mentors had noticed when they started observing our classrooms. If students are told precisely what to do and when and how, then we are depriving them of the opportunity to become self-directed, to learn how to figure things out on their own. And most importantly, to *care* about how they comport themselves. Some of the high school teachers were also advocating for student independence—and they were right.

So ten years ago we elevated the way we spoke about ideal classroom culture from respectful to respectfully independent. In the new version of our routines, students did more of the work. Now, they would be the ones to deliberate about how to build a caring community, craft a routine, write out their ideas, synthesize the best ones, self-assess and course correct, and set goals for the next day—all the things that teachers and principals had been doing.

Good teaching holds students accountable, I explained to our teachers and leaders, but great teaching leads students to hold themselves accountable. Instead of training students to behave *as if* they are focused, we should design learning experiences that are so compelling that they genuinely *are* focused.

It is relatively easy to manage students, but much harder to teach students to manage themselves. Some teachers did well, but others reverted to what they did in their old schools: sneaking in techniques like countdowns or color-coded charts. When I asked them why, they said that our approach was too difficult. Couldn't they work on independence later? After all, they said, their kids were behaving. Wasn't that the point?

And that's when it hit me. We had said that our culture would be designed around respectful independence, but we were still thinking only in terms of behavior. What we needed was a fundamental shift in the entire way we thought and talked about school culture. We needed to insist that good behavior at the expense of student agency is in fact a form of failure. We needed good behavior, while important, to be seen as a bare minimum, not the focal point. The focal point around which school culture revolved had to be student agency.

When you design systems and practices from this perspective, everything changes. I think of a little third-grade girl in a jumper and white ankle socks I noticed one day getting up from her desk to go to the supply corner. Along the way, she did a little dance with a sparkle in her eye, exuding carefree confidence. Heading back, she did the same five-second dance, disturbing no one. I smiled and thought to myself: *She is a little rebel, and I am here for it!* I flashed back to a memory of being a little rebel just like her, trying to sneak in a little dancing in elementary school. Part of great schooling is not crushing that innate spirit of independence and exuberance, which is the foundation of independent thinking and thus of intellectual sophistication.

Fostering that independence starts with structures for students to self-direct their behavior. At the beginning of the school year, we lead students through a protocol to create class commitments, which are agreements about how to self-govern their class community. "The rules that last," write Nancy and Ted Sizer, "are not arbitrarily imposed, but . . . arrived at through explanation, exploration, and persuasion."[7] A strong moral order, in other words, comes from engaging the members of a community in the rule-making process. If they create their commitments together, they will care about upholding them for one another.

Class commitments don't replace school rules. We have a complete set of strict rules—no cell phones, no tardiness, no fighting (of course), and so on—with associated consequences that are clear and consistent. And we make a point of providing students the rationale for those rules. Sometimes we ask them to determine the rationale for themselves through questions like "How does this rule help me academically or emotionally?" or "How does this rule help our school?" or "Why do you think we have this rule?" These questions help students to understand the value of the rules, and the fact that we are eliciting their thinking makes them feel respected and empowered, thus self-motivated to behave well.

The practice of formulating class commitments accomplishes this at an even deeper level. Carol Lieber explained the difference this way: "School rules are the guardrails that support an orderly environment, and they are linked to consequences. Group agreements [her term for class commitments] are aspirational and not linked to consequences. When agreements are not kept, it's time for the group to discuss what they can do to make good on them."[8]

We begin the class commitment protocol by gathering students in a circle and asking them to write responses to the following questions: "How do I want to feel at school? How do I want to be treated?" They think and write in silence for a while, then go around the circle sharing their thoughts as the teacher (or one of the students) writes their ideas on chart paper. Students in a seventh-grade class I taught one year (so we could videotape my lessons as a professional development tool for teachers) said things like "I want to feel like I fit in," "I want to feel comfortable and protected," "I want to feel like I can be myself," "Like I'm not afraid to say the wrong thing," "Like I'm important."

Next, I asked them to take a moment to look at the chart. As they gazed at their responses, it slowly dawned on them that they all wanted essentially the same thing. This awareness engendered empathy for one another, and they began to bond as a group. As they were focused on the chart, I asked: "If this is how everyone wants to feel, then *how do we need to treat each other* so that we will all feel this way?" Again I asked the students to silently think and write for a few minutes. Then we went around the circle to hear their ideas. As they spoke, I encouraged them not to reply to me but to look at and talk with one another. Some said, "We need to act mature" or "Don't laugh if someone makes a mistake." But most said something like "We need to be respectful" or "We need to be kind."

Anticipating this, I was prepared with the next question: "A lot of kids talked about respect and kindness. But those are general words. How do you know if you're being kind—what does it look and sound like? What does it really mean to be respectful; what would someone say or do?" This got the students thinking. They said things like "To be kind is to listen to someone and to care about their feelings," "Respect is like when the teacher says to do something, you do it," "Kind is never teasing, and I agree to never tease any of you," "Yeah, we need to trust each other," "Include everyone," and "Yeah, like, treat each other like a family." As they brainstormed, I could sense the feeling of intimacy that was emerging among them. Meanwhile, I wrote their ideas on a new chart titled "Class Commitments."

The next day, the students circled up again, this time to review and refine their list—eliminate redundancies, clarify language, and so on. Their sense of agency continued to grow as I asked them questions like "Does everyone agree with this edit?" Once the commitments were finalized, the next lesson was a big one. "These are your commitments to one another," I said. "They are beautiful. But right now they are still words. So now talk among yourselves and work together to figure out: How will we hold ourselves accountable to uphold our commitments? What will we do when someone breaks a commitment?" Students came up with ideas such as "We will apologize to the other person" and "We will have a discussion with the teacher." A student's outlook and comportment are transformed when they are asked to reach that level of maturity, when they are trusted to create something important.

Class commitments become moral touchstones for the students. They will reference them throughout the school year when they offer acknowledgments and apologies at the end of each school day. One afternoon, I observed this in one of our fourth-grade classrooms. "Who has an acknowledgment or apology?" the teacher asked. A boy started: "I want to apologize to Brandon. In math, I broke our commitment to not laugh when someone makes a mistake." He looked at Brandon and said, "I'm sorry." "That's okay," Brandon replied. Another student offered, "I apologize to you, John, for when we were supposed to find partners in PE and I moved away from you. I didn't mean anything bad to you, I just didn't want to be in the game." John replied, "Thank you." Last, a girl said, "Sharice, I acknowledge that you took feedback well today and made your work better."

It is incredible to see these exchanges among nine- and ten-year-olds. This protocol starts in PreK and takes place all the way through high school. Amelia, a tenth grader, started one afternoon with an apology to the teacher: "I want to apologize for giving you a hard time yesterday about that homework grade." The teacher knew that Amelia would grow more if she could take ownership of her work, so she asked, "Could you say more?" Amelia was quiet for a moment, looking down. Then she said, "Well if I'm honest, it was not my best effort.

That's on me." The teacher, having learned that not adding a comment can be powerful, nodded her head approvingly but stayed silent.

This practice of acknowledgments and apologies takes place in closing circle. The ritual of opening and closing each school day with a circle is another way we foster agency. Students sit together, looking face-to-face at one another, talking openly. In opening circle, students start by greeting one another, then take a few minutes for mindful breathing. Next, the teacher may facilitate a discussion about a social or emotional issue that she noticed cropping up the day before, leading students to talk it through to prevent a problem that might otherwise arise on social media or to avert a conflict that could create stress and become a distraction from learning. On Fridays, circles are extended to forty-five minutes to allow time for even deeper emotional interactions.

Circles helps students to feel deeply cared for and thus able to better focus on their studies. In a similar way, the practice of mindfulness empowers students to maintain emotional equilibrium, to feel calm, and thus, again, to focus on learning. Students in all our schools are given time for mindful breathing every day in every grade, from PreK through twelfth. We launch mindfulness at the beginning of each school year with lessons on brain science and the physiology of the nervous system. Students learn about neuroplasticity, the brain's ability to rewire itself, and the connection between breathing, feelings, and behavior. They come to understand when and why to employ mindful breathing. We keep it simple, with no gimmicks: just deep, slow, silent breathing. At first, teachers lead the practice. Then, after a couple of months, we teach our students to take turns leading. It's quite something to walk into a high school classroom and see the serene faces of an entire group of teenagers practicing mindful breathing, just as it is adorable to see the little ones doing it in PreK. We start our teacher and leader meetings with mindful breathing as well, to connect with inner peace.

Michael, one of our fourth graders, told me his thoughts about the practice. "Mindfulness allowed me to release the anger I had bottled up for eternity since I was born," he said. "I get angry a lot. I never had a way to do something about it. Last year I destroyed my own Lego that I had built for four months. So learning mindfulness at school, it gave me time to reflect on my emotions, and now I don't get angry as much. It gives me a second to think. I breathe in, and when I breathe in that makes me calm and not explode."

"I noticed from the first week of school that Michael was intelligent but also stubborn and angry," said his teacher, Terry Washington. "He's more advanced than the other students, but he feels self-conscious because he's into things that other students aren't. Mindfulness has helped him so much. When he gets angry, he knows to take a few minutes to breathe. He will say to me, 'I just need to breathe.' The kids understand that mindfulness is about releasing stress, releasing anxiety. I think it has made him feel better about himself."

One day I heard a ruckus in the stairwell. Some fifth graders were being rowdy coming up from recess. Instead of reprimanding them, I tried something else first. "Let's take a mindful moment. Everyone take a slow, calm, deep breath in. And a slow, calm, deep breath out." They became calm and quiet. Their mindful breathing practice had become so internalized that they were able to immediately and independently self-regulate.

In designing our school culture, we look for every opportunity, large and small, to promote student agency. We give our kindergarten students blank paper for free drawing instead of pages from coloring books. Rather than asking first-grade teachers to create nameplates for their class, we have the children create their own. They are perfectly capable of writing their names, and that simple act, for a six-year-old, is one small step of independence that helps build the foundation for drive and confidence. At the beginning of the year, instead of having teachers set up their classrooms with teacher-created decorations and commercially produced posters, as schools typically do, we start with bare walls and empty bulletin boards. The classroom becomes a blank canvas. Within days, student thinking starts to become visible. Students write about their goals and dreams, and these go up on the walls. They formulate their class commitments, and these go up on the walls. Soon, the learning environment is filled with their ideas, art, and writing.

A school's approach to discipline itself can be designed to cultivate agency. We use restorative discipline, in which students must take responsibility for their actions, understand the harm they've caused, analyze their misbehavior, and take concrete steps to "make it right" by repairing the damage they've done to the community. As the founder of the International Institute for Restorative Practices explained, "The fundamental unifying hypothesis of restorative practices is that human beings are happier, more cooperative and productive, and more likely to make positive changes in their behavior when those in positions of authority do things with them, rather than to them."[9] In other words, when they are afforded agency.

There are a number of misconceptions about restorative discipline. One is that it is unstructured. Not so. It involves different kinds of structures. Another is that *restorative* means permissive. Not at all. We have exceptionally high expectations for respect. When a teacher calls for attention, for example, we expect 100 percent of students to give their attention right away and all the way. A third is that restorative discipline is a substitute for consequences. Again, not so. Students who break a rule, such as behaving disrespectfully, will earn a consequence.

But if we do not want misbehavior to keep occurring, students need more than a consequence. They need guidance. This is the brilliance of restorative accountable discipline: It maintains consequences and then goes beyond that, teaching and inspiring students to hold themselves accountable and to take responsibility for transforming their attitudes and actions. If students misbehave, in addition to earning a consequence, we have them engage in reflection and writing. The process has five steps, each with specific questions in a deliberate sequence.[10] The first step is getting the story out. This is important, because students, especially adolescents, when they feel angry, have a hard time focusing on how to improve. Questions include "Describe in detail what happened and your role in what happened." Then, "What words describe how you are feeling?" (Some options are provided, including "angry," "sad," "depressed," "frustrated," "confused," and "embarrassed," followed by "Why do you feel this way?") By taking a few minutes to identify how he or she is feeling and getting a chance to express in writing his or her version of the story, the student has a chance to let off steam and feel validated. This step has a calming and focusing effect, and the student is now in a mindset to be productive.

The next step is taking responsibility. Questions include "How did your actions impact your learning?" "In what ways did your behavior impact others?" and "What rules or expectations did you violate?" Third comes problem-solving and moving forward. The key question here is "When a situation like this comes up again, what do you want to pay attention to and do?" This question implies a high level of respect for the student and inspires him or her to want to live up to that respect. The fourth step is preparation and rehearsal. Here the question is "What might be some things you can say or do to restore your good standing in class and repair your relationship with the teacher and/or your peers?" This is where the student drafts what he or she will say and/or do upon returning to class, and the dean may provide feedback and coaching as the student rehearses this. (Depending on the severity of the infraction, the student may not be allowed to return to class that period or even for the rest of the day.) The fifth and final step is getting support and keeping on track. The student addresses two questions: "What are two to three things that you can do to stay on track? What are one or two things that your teacher(s) might do to support you?" Figuring out how to get help for oneself is a key component of agency and a skill that students will need in college.

Once all this is done, the student is asked if he or she is truly ready. "Take some time and really look over what you have said. Ask yourself if your teacher will think you put 100 percent effort into your work. Get yourself ready to explain how you will fix your behavior so that you can return to class." This entire process—going through the steps, considering how one's actions affected others, strategizing and planning how to improve—reflects the central role of agency in restorative discipline. At the same time, the teacher's authority is respected, and the student understands that we do not accept second-rate work of any kind, including with regard to behavior and discipline. In light of this, the teacher will review the student's answers, hear anything that he or she has to say, and decide whether to accept the student back into class.

Ultimately, restorative practices support students to fulfill their innate potential. David is a high school senior who started at HVA in fifth grade. "I was living in the Bronx, surrounded by a lot of negative influences," David said. "I was hanging outside with friends who were much older than me. There was a lot of violence. I lost a few good friends." His mom was working the evening shift at the city housing authority.

"He is such an impressive young man," said Yohana. "Very polished, sharp. His shirt is the whitest shirt of all the students. He's very respectful. But—" Yohana continued, "his desire to be the best means that if he doesn't get his way, if he believes someone has disrespected him in any way, he can get very confrontational."

We do not allow cell phones at school. Students hand them in each morning at the front door. "One morning David told me that he didn't have his phone," Yohana said. "But later that day he got caught with it. The teacher confiscated it, and the dean, Henry, locked it up. After school. David thought that somehow he could sweet-talk Henry into giving it back. Of course, Henry told him that he would be calling his mother and she'd have to pick it up. David stormed downstairs. A student who saw him asked, 'Are you okay?' He pushed her aside and started yelling at me, 'I need my phone! Can I get my phone? Can I get my phone?' I said, 'You know the rules,' but before I could add anything, he turned around and went back upstairs to Henry's office."

"He burst into my office," Henry said. "He was yelling at the top of his lungs, 'This is not fair! Give me my fucking phone! It's *my* fucking property!' I told him to have a seat, and I went to close the door, but he blocked the door with his foot. Then he slammed his fist into the door. 'Give me my fucking phone!' Yohana came up to let me know what had happened downstairs. I called David's mother to let her know that he had earned a suspension for egregious disrespect."

Three days later, David returned to school for his restorative meeting with Henry. "I asked him, 'Why do you think you got to that place of belligerence?' And his reply was 'I don't even remember half of what I did.' I've known him a long time, so I knew he was sincere. I went over all that happened, and as he heard it, he put his face in his hands. He was really upset with himself. I went on, 'If you get this angry every time something doesn't go your way, what will happen in your life?' And he said, 'People will not want to help me. I'll push people away. They won't see me for who I am. I don't know why I flip out when I get mad.' He could see that he was getting in his own way."

David is exceptionally bright. That self-awareness and introspection were precisely what the restorative process is designed to elicit.

Henry continued, "I said to him, 'You have a learned behavior that you need to unlearn.' He was really interested. He asked me, 'How do I do that?' I suggested that when he gets angry, he can take a pause. I could see that he really cared. 'But when I'm in that angry moment, how can I pause?' he asked. 'When that happens,' I said, 'you can tell the teacher that you're getting upset and you need a moment. Ask to be excused. Then come to my office.' So, from that discussion, when he was upset, he would replace the outburst with the new habit of showing up in my office to sit down and breathe for a minute, get himself together."

Meanwhile, David still had to restore his relationships with multiple people. He went to each person he had hurt. He went to the friend he'd pushed out of the way and said, "I'm really sorry, but I'm not just apologizing. I'm working on myself." He also went to Yohana for a restorative meeting. "I realize that I have a problem," he told her. "You don't deserve the way I was speaking to you. I'm sorry that I didn't treat you right. If I'm going to be the man I want to be, and keep having all these opportunities the school gives me, I know I can't do that."

"When I returned to school, I felt reminded of my potential," David said. "The school counselor recommended that I apply for a Columbia University precollege program. HVA offers us these summer opportunities, but I didn't know if it was for someone like me. When I was accepted, I felt proud. Ecstatic, really. But also unsure of my place at a school like Columbia. My program was called Freedom & Citizenship based on the core curriculum at Columbia. We studied great thinkers like Plato, Socrates, and Frederick Douglass in a seminar format. We did a reenactment of *The Trial and Death of Socrates*. I was Socrates! We read the Constitution." David said that the discussions outside of class were just as important as the discussion in class. "Now I have a friend from Germany, a friend from China. I met one student who was particularly extraordinary. I saw Kyle's dedication to his own future. I now have a new mantra: Be like Kyle! I saw how hard people were working. It made me reexamine my life." David just graduated and started his freshman year at a selective four-year college.

•

These practices and structures—a culture of caring, student-created routines, class commitments, opening and closing circles, mindfulness, restorative discipline—they all cultivate agency. When students have agency, they don't just follow directions, they care about being a kind person; they don't just do their assignments, they care about the quality of their work.

The results can be remarkable. Consider our morning routine:

Twenty-six kindergarteners are working independently as the school day begins in a classroom that radiates the soft hum of carefree childhood activity. The children are at once serious and serene. Several are looking at vocabulary words on the wall; one little boy is delivering plastic supply bins to each table; others are reading books or playing with blocks.

The teacher rings a chime. The class falls silent and looks at her. "Time to make our way to opening circle," she says. The children start buzzing about, pushing in chairs, putting away papers, helping one another tidy up. The teacher spots two of them bickering. She does not issue demerits or change their behavior chart from green to yellow, nor does she solve their conflict for them. Instead, she walks over and firmly asks a guiding question—"How do you think you should handle this?"—and they figure out how to resolve the conflict for themselves.

Meanwhile, the class has gathered in a circle on the rug, chatting and giggling as children do. The rug is solid blue, without squares or circles (a decision we made so students would learn to independently navigate social norms). The last two kids approach the rug, but there is no room for them in the circle. The teacher stays silent, knowing what we taught about student self-management. Sure enough, the other kids shift around to make space for the latecomers, and the class reforms itself into a circle. A boy and girl stand up, beaming. They are this week's circle leaders, a coveted classroom job. As they walk over to two tiny chairs by an easel, the class quiets down and looks at them. "Good morning," the girl says to her classmates. She and the boy proceed to lead opening circle.

This morning routine, which might appear to consist of a series of minor miracles, was made possible by the agency-centered design we had undertaken in painstaking detail, and by the innate potential of the students themselves.

8.

Ethical Purpose

A truly exceptional education, finally, addresses the larger matters of ethics and purpose, leading students to examine society and self, to cultivate an abiding inner life, and to begin to discern their calling.

School should be a place where students find fellowship within an intellectual community that instills a reverence for knowledge and meaning. Where studying the world's greatest books, ideas, and thinkers provides a grounding for one's life. "There is more in us than we know," educator Kurt Hahn said. "If we can be made to see it, perhaps for the rest of our lives we will be unwilling to settle for less."[1] School should guide students to internalize this mindset.

But nothing could be further from the experience of students in most schools, where they are confronted with a deeply flawed system of credits, extra credit, and class ranking that dominates the culture. The system compels students, especially high school students, to employ a sort of gamesmanship—focusing on what will "count" for credit, raising hands to appear interested, currying favor with teachers, studying only what will be on the test, taking shortcuts to get good grades, contesting grades. For younger students, there are huge boxes of test-prep toys and prizes, along with test-prep effort parties, test-prep bulletin boards with each child's score posted, and test-prep speeches to "pump up" the children. Then, for some godforsaken reason, it all culminates in pep rallies that place the state test on a pedestal as the pinnacle of the school year. Can you imagine such a spectacle at Exeter or Trinity? It is obscene.

These practices have serious implications. I have heard students talk about reading not in terms of ideas, knowledge, or the beauty of the literature but as a thing you do to get a score.

Then there is the daily influence of American culture: the obsession with money, possessions, glamour, status, and celebrity. Indeed, some schools now advise students to "develop your brand." Have we so completely lost our compass that we would encourage children to see themselves not as souls to be refined but as brands to be promoted, to regard their lives in the most trivial way possible?

After thirteen years steeped in this culture, students become conditioned to see scores and prizes as the sine qua non of educational achievement. They can't help but care more about grades than the sophistication of their own thinking, more about awards than knowledge, more about class rank than discovering the mysteries of the universe.

Students do not come to these conclusions on their own but because, as William Deresiewicz says, "a constellation of values is ceaselessly inculcated" by the educational system.[2] These values are manifested in what we teach and how we teach but, most fundamentally, in the *experience* of school. What does that experience compel students to do and think? What does school convey to them, explicitly and tacitly, about the purpose of their education and, by extension, of their lives? Philip Jackson called this the hidden curriculum: the values implicitly communicated to students through the daily routines and structures of school.[3]

How should we transmit, instead, the values that we care about, or at the very least teach students to critically question ephemeral values like prestige and popularity? How should we teach them to pursue a purposeful life? I do not understand purpose reductively as a college major or career but as a calling, a defining vision for one's life. As Rilke said, "Ask yourself in the stillest hour of the night: *Must I?* If you meet this solemn question with a strong and simple 'I must,' then build your life according to this necessity; your life even unto its slightest and most indifferent hour must be a sign of this urge and a testimony to it."[4]

We return here to the three elements of the Graduate Profile.

First, when students learn to think analytically about the material they encounter in school, they can apply this critical thinking to all that they encounter outside of school—the commercialism, the political ideologies, the shallow presentation of what passes for news, the vapid content on social media. When students are well-read, acquainted with important facts and ideas, and immersed in quality books, they come to possess a base of knowledge and a vantage point from which to question the information, or misinformation, that others are trying to sell them.

Second, when students develop agency with respect to their work in school, it transfers over into their lives. Once students experience what it feels like to take ownership of their studies, they will look for that feeling in everything they do. They won't be satisfied with going through the motions or chasing external rewards. They become people of substance, self-possessed rather than self-absorbed.

Then, we need to teach students to use these skills for a worthy purpose. Over the course of thirteen years at school, surely we can provide time for them to consider how they want to use their lives. Students need the opportunity to stop and look up from the day-to-day in order to develop the capacity for moral reasoning and to think about why they were put on this earth.

Foundational to the development of ethical purpose is the opportunity to think about who you are and what it means to be a moral individual. At Sidwell Friends, students have regular time for silent reflection. At Kurt Hahn's schools, they had projects for exploration and nature walks for quiet thinking. At my summer camp, we had discussion groups in which we were taught to consider our lives in relation to our responsibility to be upstanding people. And at HVA, we have an advisory system that is built into the rhythm of the school year.

In advisory, fifth through twelfth graders are divided into groups of about twelve, each led by a teacher. The idea is for every student to have at least one caring adult who knows that student very well, provides guidance and personal attention, and serves as a point person for parents.[5] Each advisory group becomes like a small "family" within the school. This gives students a warm, nurturing feeling of belonging that can counter the alienation and loneliness so many feel. Advisory provides the one certain time and place for students to connect with one another, for the teacher to connect personally with them, and for students to think and talk about a purposeful approach to school and life.

Advisory can guide students to grow, year by year, from preadolescent to poised young adult. It can be a chance for students to discuss ideas related to character and ethics—to engage in philosophical interrogation of ethical issues, to encounter questions like "Why is it important to act with integrity even if no one is looking?" and "What values are essential to the public good in a liberal democratic society and why?" Discussing such questions in a sustained way enables students to become individuals who will lead thoughtful lives.

It's important, too, that students learn about the problems and issues of the day and think about how they themselves might be of service. Opportunities for service learning can be structured into advisory, with rich experiences and lots of choices at every step so that students are driving the process. This will lead them to approach their service projects with intrinsic motivation rather than looking at service as a way to enhance their college resumes. Those choices, for younger students, can be simple. When planning a holiday giving project, for instance, a class can vote on whether to collect canned food, coats, socks, or toys, and on how to design the posters. For older students, the process can be more elaborate, beginning with studying local and global problems, choosing an issue to research and work on, meeting with experts in the field, planning and organizing, then evaluating and possibly writing about the results.

One year, a number of our high school seniors said they were concerned about drug trafficking in Harlem. Many older kids would drop off their little siblings or cousins at our elementary school down the block. "I bring my first-grade cousin to school in the morning," one student said. "I don't want her to see people knocked out on drugs as she walks to school, people lying flat on the sidewalk at eight o'clock in the morning." In advisory and in conversations after school with teachers, the students talked about the lack of safety in the neighborhood. "We don't want the freshmen influenced by the drug dealers across the street," one senior said. "They're selling K2 in the park and in the delis." An advisor connected him and his friends with an anti-drug nonprofit. Soon the students were making public service announcement videos. Before long, they were invited to a conference in Washington, DC, meeting elected officials and learning how to address drug issues within the community.

Advisory can also help students to develop a sense of purpose in relation to their schoolwork, which can lead them to begin to discern their purpose in a broader sense. We set this process in motion right at the beginning of the school year by asking students to write about what they envision for themselves, what some of their goals or intentions are for the year. The impact is profound as this exercise effects a kind of paradigm shift in their attitude. They go from just following along to taking the lead. What *do* I want for myself? One year, a student wrote, "My goal is to get better at writing." Another wrote, "My intention for this school year is to never give up no matter how hard things get." There can be one goal for academics and one for study habits; there can be a vision for the year followed by an intention for the first week. The details are less important than the fact that students are being asked to think—really think—about the purpose of all the things they do in school. After they write their first drafts, we ask, "Why are these goals important to you?" Then, "How will you go about achieving them?" and "Looking back from your last day of school, how will you know you've achieved them?" Students quietly reflect and write more; then, in the company of classmates, they talk it all through.

Starting the year this way cultivates confidence and maturity and changes the way that students perceive themselves. But these qualities need to be developed and reinforced throughout the year. Recognizing that, we instituted the Student-Led Learning Cycle. Guided by their advisors, students start the cycle each Friday. They determine their goals for the upcoming week and design plans for how to achieve them. During the week, they self-manage their work and track their progress using dedicated notebooks. They push themselves because they are working toward goals *they* designed. At the end of the week, they think about the results, then self-assess and write. How well am I doing in meeting my goals? Should I revise the strategies I'm using? Fellow students offer peer critique. Should you change the way you're going about this? Is there a more effective approach? The last step of the cycle feeds back into the next iteration. Students revise their goals for the following week, formulate the next step, or decide they are ready to move on to a new goal.

The larger idea—with advisory, with setting intentions for the year, with the weekly cycle of student-led learning—is that when students develop a sense of purpose in school, it will eventually transfer to their lives. What kind of person do I want to be? What is my vision for myself? What will be my unique contribution to the world? You're fifteen, and from the very first day of school, someone is asking you what you think about your life. You listen as your peers grapple with the same questions, and you all come out with different answers. The experience leaves an indelible impression, giving you a glimpse of what is possible. You have not necessarily determined your purpose yet, but you understand that purpose is a thing. And you arrive at a place where you cannot imagine living anything less than a soulful, purposeful life.

CONCLUSION

The Only Hope Society Has

In the eight years since I started working on this book, raising well-educated children has become more challenging. Public discourse has become more superficial, culture more intolerant, social media more harmful. Schools have changed in ways that many parents find disconcerting. Childhood itself is increasingly fraught.

In such difficult times, we are called to focus intently on the quality of our children's education.

I am reminded of the words of a Hasidic rabbi whose writings I studied in college: "We have two basic assurances. The first is that one action is worth more than a thousand sighs. And second, that no action for a good purpose has ever been done in vain. In the long run, it will succeed and pay its dividends."[1] We need to be clear about our purpose and work as hard as we can, and when we are distraught, we need to keep focused and keep working. We can be sure that the labor and love we invest in our children and our schools will pay off.

So what, specifically, can parents, educators, and policymakers do?

First, while there are many important elements of a good education, quality teaching is the most consequential. "Exhortations to improve students' higher order thinking abilities accomplish little without able teachers who know how to support challenging learning," writes Linda Darling-Hammond. "The bottom line is that there is just no way to create good schools without good teachers."[2] Quality teaching should be the central organizing principle of education policy.

But teaching is more difficult than most people understand. Imagine being responsible for keeping an entire classroom of young people engaged for five hours a day, each and every day, asking students meaningful and challenging questions, giving effective feedback that will inspire students to care about the quality of their work, assigning and grading homework, selecting books that will spark each student's interest, providing accelerated work for those who are capable of more challenge while tutoring those who need extra help, spending time with those who need emotional support, dealing effectively with misbehavior, participating in faculty meetings, monitoring dismissal or lunch, covering a class for a colleague who is suddenly not feeling well, practicing lockdown drills, mediating student disagreements, investing time in your own professional development, and staying in communication with parents. Aren't you tired just reading all of that?

And teaching for deeper learning is even more difficult. Teachers need to become what Darling-Hammond calls "adaptive experts" who are capable of discerning precisely "what the problems are when students are not learning, and adapting materials, teaching strategies, or supports accordingly."[3] Doing this well requires teachers to possess exceptional judgment, subject-area knowledge, and pedagogical expertise.

Schools therefore must set as high a bar as possible for who gets hired. In every school in America, it should be exceptionally competitive and challenging to secure a position as a teacher. Teaching should be the most coveted and prestigious role in society. Becoming a teacher should be like becoming a doctor. Teachers should receive four years of postgraduate education, and just as new MDs spend several years as interns and residents, so should newly graduated teachers spend several years apprenticing in classrooms under the tutelage of master teachers. New teachers need models, and they need to live the details, day in and day out, before they are entrusted with a classroom of their own. I've seen new teachers who had all the potential in the world, but thrown into a classroom by themselves, they never became very good. I've seen others who were lucky enough to be placed in a room with an exceptional veteran teacher. Within a couple of years, they were doing the things their mentor did and teaching incredibly well. Like all practitioners, teachers tend to get better with experience, so every school needs enough veteran teachers to support those coming up.

In order for this to be possible, we need to create the conditions for teachers to remain in the profession for the long term. The way that my colleagues and I worked twelve-hour days during our early years is not sustainable or scalable. As a nation, if we want our children to have what they truly need, we must pay teachers like doctors and invest in reasonable staff-to-student ratios and extensive, ongoing professional development.

But none of this will produce the great schools that our country needs without robust accountability at every level, from teachers to principals to district leaders. An effective system of accountability, while complicated to design, is indispensable for effective schooling. So is a *culture* of accountability, where teachers are so respected and supported that they hold themselves accountable. Such a culture attracts smart, talented individuals, who want to work alongside others who are equally gifted.

Parents, of course, can have a substantial influence on their children's education through a considered approach to parenting.

When our children were growing up, my husband Joel and I were unable, like most parents, to afford private school. Instead, we did our best to fill in the gaps in their education. We wanted them to be sophisticated, independent thinkers. Joel would talk and joke with them at a level far above their age so they had to be sharp to keep up. I'd say over and over, "Don't believe everything you read. Even if it's in *The New York Times.*" And because we did not want our children to absorb the superficial, materialistic values of the surrounding culture, we taught them to be skeptical of whatever messages were coming at them. Standing in line at the grocery store, I'd ask, "Look at that magazine cover; why do you think the girls have so much makeup on? What are they trying to sell?" We also wanted them to be considerate of others and to care about the greater good. We taught them to always give part of their allowance to charity. "It's only really giving if you give more than you are comfortable with," I'd say. Once a month, we made bagged lunches for the homeless. We could have just donated to the organization, but we wanted the kids to do the work: shop in the store, make the sandwiches, boil the eggs, write little notes, pack the bags, and deliver them.

Of course, we wanted them to be avid readers. They were not required to read much at school, so we had them read extensively at home. We put bookshelves in every room (including the kitchen) and filled the house with high-quality books missing from the school curriculum. On the weekends, we went to the library or bookstore, and on Sunday nights we all read together. We did not allow TV (except for football and baseball) until fifth grade, and then only one show per week. That left plenty of time for reading, as well as for hobbies, puzzles, music, crafts, and lots of playing outside. We wanted to protect the joy and wholesomeness of their childhood.

Parents can also vote for policymakers who will put the needs of children above the pressures of special interests. The philosopher John Rawls said that the way to design a fair society is through a "veil of ignorance"—to start by imagining that you do not know the circumstances into which you will be born. That is the approach we need to take to education policy. We should ask our elected officials: if *your* children were assigned by blind lottery to any public school—putting them at risk of attending the worst—what policies would you enact? You can be sure they would swiftly support ideas that have transformative potential, like performance assessment, charter schools, and accountability, along with higher pay for teachers.

Perhaps the biggest impediment to transformation is the fact that American public education has been stuck in a chronic reinvention of the wheel. Each generation seems to discover the same problems anew, apparently unaware of the immense body of work that has come before—ideas that were conceived, developed, documented, and implemented, often with great effect.

Vito Perrone was for many years a leading educator and the founder of the legendary North Dakota Study Group. In one of his celebrated annual talks, he said, "We should all exert caution every time we hear that something related to schools is new. It usually means that those speaking of the new haven't chosen to examine the historical record."[4]

As Grant Wiggins wrote, "Is there NO memory in this field? Are we to assume that each new crop of teachers knows nothing . . . are we doomed to reinvent the wheel in every classroom every generation? None of this is new and it insults the intelligence to make it sound new."[5] And Donna Santman said, "It's like Groundhog Day! We're having *this* conversation again. And how many times will we have *this* conversation?"

Even a cursory review of the history of education shows that many if not most of the concepts recently promoted as new and innovative were in fact conceived twenty, fifty, even one hundred years ago or more. To cite just a few examples, serious educators have long understood that the application of knowledge is central to deep thinking, that intrinsic motivation enhances academic achievement, that free play is essential to intellectual and emotional development, that students should be immersed in the world's great books, that emotion drives cognition (when students feel cared for and connected, they do better in school), and that persistence is best taught by giving students experiences that call upon them to persist.

Socrates taught through inquiry, discourse, and the questioning of conventional thinking. John Dewey wrote about intrinsic motivation.[6] W.E.B. DuBois advocated for a liberal arts curriculum for students of color.[7] Maria Montessori pioneered self-direction in learning.[8] In the 1950s, Jerome Bruner ignited a revolution in cognitive science, elucidating the importance of discovery and agency in the classroom.[9] In 1960, the architects of the International Baccalaureate, influenced by Dewey, Bruner, and the child psychologist Jean Piaget, established the foundation of the IB to focus on reasoning and critical analysis rather than memorization.[10] In 1968, James P. Comer explained how social-emotional learning was essential to a child's development[11] and garnered national attention for the idea of "bringing all the adults together to support children's growth."[12] In 1985, Debbie Meier formulated her "Habits of Mind," which included teaching students to cite evidence for claims.[13] In 1988, leading educational thinkers at Harvard designed the "Teach for Understanding" framework, emphasizing the transfer of knowledge and skills, the idea of teaching students "to think and act flexibly with what one knows."[14] In 1994, Linda Darling-Hammond led a commission that produced one of the most influential education reports of the decade, *What Matters Most: Teaching for America's Future*, on the importance of teacher quality as a precondition for deeper learning.[15] In 1999, the seminal work on learning science, *How People Learn*, explained, among other findings, the role of metacognition in learning. And for half a century, the late, great Ted Sizer "changed the way people all over the world now think and speak of school,"[16] advancing some of the most compelling practices known to educators today, including curricular depth, performance assessment, advisory, project-based learning, and demonstration of mastery through portfolios and exhibitions.[17]

Clearly we do not need to reimagine education so much as we need the humility to learn from and build on the work of those who have come before us.

"The purpose of education," James Baldwin wrote, "is to create in a person the ability to look at the world for himself, to make his own decisions." So, he continued, "The obligation of anyone who thinks of himself as responsible is to examine society and try to change it and to fight it—at no matter what risk. This is the only hope society has."[18]

Imagine how magnificent it will be when we are educating our children to become independent, curious, driven, knowledgeable, humble, compassionate young people and sending them out to bring kindness and light into the world.

This is the task of the next generation.

ACKNOWLEDGMENTS

This book is a testament to the educators I've had the honor of working with and learning from over the years. Thank you to the extraordinary teachers, principals, staff, advisors, and school leaders whose work has informed the ideas in this book. A special thank you to our beloved families at HVA for your partnership. And most of all, thank you to our precious students—I am deeply proud of you.

My heartfelt gratitude to our community of supporters, including our incredible board of directors, trustees, donors, and volunteers. Thank you for sustaining our mission and caring so much about our children.

Thank you to my gifted, brilliant editor, Molly Stern, for your masterful editing and passionate advocacy for this book, and to the dedicated team at Zando, including the wonderful Sarah Goldstein, Sam Mitchell, Nathalie Ramirez, and Andrew Rein. I appreciate each and every one of you.

My humble gratitude to John Legend. Thank you for your enduring commitment to educational excellence and for publishing this book with Get Lifted Books. I am grateful for your valuable ideas and insights and your belief in our shared vision. Thank you to Mike Jackson and the fabulous team at Get Lifted Film Co., including MacKenzie Marlowe and Richard Foster-Shelton. Thank you to Ty Stiklorius and the magnificent Friends at Work team.

Acknowledgments

Thank you to the colleagues and friends who provided critical feedback over the years. To Bill Deresiewicz, a special thank you for your incisive critique and remarkable editorial talent.

My deepest thanks to the late, great Bob Barnett for always looking out for me and for caring fiercely about this project, and to Ellis Levine for your wise counsel. Thank you to the wonderful team at WME, including Jay Mandel, Howard Yoon, Caroline Cox, and Morgan Montgomery.

Thank you to Kenneth Gillett, Lindsay Carter, and the TMD team, including Krasimir Galabov, Gonzaga Gómez-Cortázar Romero, Amy Duncan, Megan Kramer, Aaron Gaines, Sahil Dhaliwal, and Marisa Rifici for your consummate professionalism, high-quality work, and advice. To Jesse Dylan, Priscilla Cohen, and the magnificent team at Wondros, thank you for your inspired, creative work. Thank you to Paul Sliker for your expertise and belief in the importance of this book.

I would like to thank my parents for instilling in me the values that became the foundation of my life, chief among them the importance of being kind and helpful to others, a central tenet of our Jewish faith. And thank you to my entire family and to all my friends for your abiding support and love.

Finally, thank you to my children. You are the most important thing in my life. I am so proud of each of you. Thank you for your love and encouragement, your candid feedback, and for bringing me so much joy.

NOTES

INTRODUCTION

1. Thomas J. Kane and Douglas O. Staiger, *Gathering Feedback for Teaching: Combining High-Quality Observations with Student Surveys and Achievement Gains* (Bill & Melinda Gates Foundation, January 2012). The study examined important aspects of high-level teaching and learning, such as problem-solving, content understanding, analysis, and quality of feedback.
2. Julia Moeller, Marc A. Brackett, Zorana Ivcevic, and Arielle E. White, Yale Center for Emotional Intelligence, "High School Students' Feelings: Discoveries from a Large National Survey and an Experience Sampling Study," *Learning and Instruction* 66 (April 2020). The study also found that 75 percent of students have negative feelings about school.
3. The commissioner of the National Center for Education Statistics, Peggy Carr, said the NAEP results for the US were devastating and the results of the Trends in International Mathematics and Science Study (TIMSS) assessment, an international study of 650,000 students from sixty-four countries, were "just as devastating," calling these "sharp, steep declines."
4. Debbie Meier, in discussion with the author, November 22, 2017. In December 2022, Larry Rosenstock said something similar: "None of us has gotten there. We all keep reaching."

Notes

CHAPTER 1

1. Isaiah Berlin, *Two Concepts of Liberty: An Inaugural Lecture Delivered Before the University of Oxford on October 31, 1958,* (Clarendon Press, 1958).
2. Tom Hayden et al., "Port Huron Statement," Students for a Democratic Society, June 1962.
3. Jack Kerouac, *On the Road* (Viking Press, 1957).

CHAPTER 2

1. Jonathan Kozol, *Amazing Grace: The Lives of Children and the Conscience of a Nation* (Crown Publishers, 1995).
2. Students of Gary and Jerri-Ann Jacobs High Tech High, *San Diego Bay: A Call for Conservation*, foreword by E. O. Wilson, preface by Jane Goodall (University of California San Diego Sea Grant Program, 2009).
3. Howard Fuller, *No Struggle, No Progress: A Warrior's Life from Black Power to Education Reform* (Marquette University Press, 2014).
4. The charter movement was also focused on addressing educational inequality based on class and race. The nation's first charter school law was passed in Minnesota on June 4, 1991. For an interesting overview of the origins of charter schools, see "Where Did Charter Schools Come From?" by Chester E. Finn Jr. and Brandon L. Wright in *Education Next*, May 4, 2016. Ray Budde had published a paper describing a form of chartering in 1974 and another paper in 1988; the latter was cited in a speech by Albert Shanker. Finn and Wright explain that this influenced the group in Minnesota, including Joe Nathan, Ted Kolderie, Curtis Johnson, and Democratic State Senator Ember Reichgott. They "encountered fierce opposition" and twice failed.

5. The nation's first charter school, City Academy, opened in St. Paul in 1992. The nation's second charter school (the first in California), San Carlos Charter Learning Center, was founded by Don Shalvey in 1992.
6. Aspire was founded in 1998 by Don together with Netflix founder Reed Hastings. The idea was to create a school district of sorts comprised of charter schools, both to educate as many students as possible and to produce the economies of scale to do so. According to Don, this was not permitted until he and Reed lobbied to change the California state charter law in 1998.
7. The history of education in Harlem has been one of inequity, as the community has been underserved. As described in *Educating Harlem*, "At no point in the twentieth century did a majority of Black Harlem residents enjoy confidence that their children would receive decent, sufficient, and equitable schooling. But many Harlem community members from diverse identity and ideological positions labored, theorized, imagined, organized, and built toward this goal. Their efforts . . . were highly consequential." Ansley T. Erickson and Ernest Morrell, eds., *Educating Harlem: A Century of Schooling and Resistance in a Black Community* (Columbia University Press, 2019), 10.
8. Nancie Atwell, *The Reading Zone: How to Help Kids Become Skilled, Passionate, Habitual, Critical Readers* (Scholastic, 2007).
9. Paul Lockhart, *A Mathematician's Lament: How School Cheats Us Out of Our Most Fascinating and Imaginative Art Form* (Bellevue Literary Press, 2009).
10. New York State Education Department, 2007–2008. Ranking of all nonselective New York State public schools, both district and charter.
11. New York State Education Department, 2008; includes all nonselective high schools.

12. Letters to state official from US Congressman Charles Rangel, chairman of the Committee on Ways and Means, June 23, 2008, and from Harlem Community Board 10 chairman W. Franc Perry, May 27, 2008.
13. White House Archives, "President Bush Encourages the Reauthorization of No Child Left Behind," April 24, 2007.
14. United States Secretary of Education Arne Duncan, *Morning Joe*, March 15, 2009.
15. Michael Bloomberg, "Harlem's Amazing Charter," *New York Post*, March 12, 2009.
16. "The 2010 O Power List," *O, The Oprah Magazine*, September 14, 2010.
17. Joe Klein, "Teaching Accountability," *Time*, March 1, 2011.

CHAPTER 3

1. Grant Wiggins and Jay McTighe, *Understanding by Design* (Association for Supervision and Curriculum Development, 2005).
2. Donna Santman, *Shades of Meaning: Comprehension and Interpretation in Middle School* (Heinemann, 2005), 49–50.
3. Ron Berger, *An Ethic of Excellence: Building a Culture of Craftsmanship with Students* (Heinemann, 2003).
4. Richard Elmore famously studied and wrote about District 2 in several reports with Deanna Burney, including "Staff Development and Instructional Improvement in Community School District #2, New York City" for the National Commission on Teaching and America's Future and the Consortium for Policy Research in Education (1996); "School Variation and Systemic Instructional Improvement in Community School District #2, New York City" for the High Performance Learning Communities Project (1997);

and "Continuous Improvement in Community District #2" (1998).

5. Shelley Harwayne, *Going Public: Priorities & Practice at the Manhattan New School* (Heinemann, 1999). The Manhattan New School was a public elementary school known as "the free Ethical Culture" due to its private school-level quality. Shelley had advised countless teachers, principals, and superintendents throughout the world. The book is an account of her work at the school, and she shares both philosophical ideas as well as practical advice and resources on school leadership.
6. Sadly, after two years together, Grant would not get to see that long game with us. Upon his untimely passing in 2015, we hosted a memorial service with his family at our high school that was attended by people from around the country.
7. The very first Reggio Emilia preschool was opened in 1860 by the citizens of the city of Reggio Emilia in northern Italy. In the 1960s, early childhood educator Loris Malaguzzi contributed to and codified the approach. In 1981, Malaguzzi conceived of the idea of an exhibition that took place in Reggio Emilia, showcasing preschool-student projects and teacher ideas and stories. Originally called "If the Eye Leaps over the Wall: Hypotheses for Visionary Didactics," it was subsequently titled "The Hundred Languages of Children: A Narrative of the Possible" (named for a celebrated poem by Malaguzzi). The exhibition made its way around the world, and with it, educators met to discuss early childhood pedagogy. This eventually culminated in the development of more structured international networks of support for Reggio Emilia schools. See *The Hundred Languages of Children: The Reggio Emilia Experience in Transformation*, Carolyn Edwards, Lella Gandini, and George Forman, eds. (Praeger, 1993).

8. Bob Dylan in *No Direction Home*, directed by Martin Scorsese, aired on September 27, 2005, as part of the *American Masters* series on PBS.
9. There were all kinds of connections to Ted and Debbie. Grant referred to Debbie as his hero and named his concept of essential questions in homage to Ted's Coalition of Essential Schools (Grant Wiggins, in discussion with the author, October 30, 2013). Debbie's grandchildren had attended Shelley's school. Dennis said that "Ted and Debbie believed in my work when most didn't." Howard Fuller said he learned from Ted about the value of small schools. Ted and Debbie were also the first people that Ron mentioned when asked about his own mentors. Ron had worked in Cambridge with Steve Seidel, whose mother, Adria Steinberg, had worked with Larry, who had developed his school design for High Tech High in Cambridge with Howard, Dennis, and, of course, Ted and Debbie. From 1995 through 1997, Ted, Debbie, Howard, Larry, and Dennis traveled around the country visiting high schools. They had, as Larry called it, a "war room" in Cambridge where they synthesized all the ideas gathered during their observations. Larry said that many of these ideas informed the foundation of his design of High Tech High a few years later (Larry Rosenstock, in discussion with the author, July 14, 2016). Ted had recruited Howard to become a senior fellow at the Annenberg Institute for School Reform at Brown University. Howard said, "Ted gave me a framework to make the distinction between public education and the system that delivers it" (Howard Fuller, in correspondence with the author, March 19, 2023).
10. This major national project involved Ted and a group of colleagues visiting eighty schools. The study was cosponsored by the National Association of Secondary School Principals and the Commission on Educational Issues of the National Association of Independent Schools. It culminated in the

publication of the celebrated *Horace's Compromise: The Dilemma of the American High School* (Houghton Mifflin, 1984) as well as *The Shopping Mall High School: Winners and Losers in the Educational Marketplace* by Arthur G. Powell, Eleanor Farrar, and David K. Cohen (Houghton Mifflin, 1985) and *The Last Little Citadel: American High Schools Since 1940* by Robert Hampel (Houghton Mifflin, 1986).

11. Dennis said that after attending a lecture by Ted on school improvement, he went up to Ted and blurted out, "All your radical ideas—you're just talking about it, I'm doing it. Get your ass down to my school!" Ted did so, and that's how Dennis's school became the first in the coalition.

12. Debbie Meier, in discussion with the author, April 13, 2018. The inequality in American public education was documented by Joseph Mayer Rice in *The Public-School System of the United States* (Century, 1893). This investigative report famously exposed the dismal state of public schools, describing them as "dehumanizing institutions" that trained students with "sing-song drill, rote repetition, and meaningless verbiage." While the sons of the elite studied the classics to prepare for college and positions of leadership, most children were trained to follow orders. According to Lawrence Cremin (in *The Transformation of the School: Progressivism in American Education, 1876–1957* [Vintage, 1961]), Rice originally wrote this "firsthand appraisal of American schools" for a series in a New York monthly called *The Forum* after visiting thirty-six cities and talking with over a thousand public school teachers. The report explained that schools were run by the political establishment, which hired untrained teachers. Rice also noted some rare "bright spots," such as Francis Parker's "world-famous" progressive school.

13. Debbie Meier, *The Power of Their Ideas: Lessons for America from a Small School in Harlem* (Beacon Press, 2002), 4. For her part, Debbie said the people she learned from were Ted Sizer, Lillian Weber, Mike Harrington, and Vito Perrone.

14. Debbie Meier, in discussion with the author, November 24, 2017.
15. Debbie Meier, in discussion with the author, June 3, 2019, and August 18, 2021. Her team used this framework as the foundation for designing their curriculum and instruction. She also said the Habits of Mind were based on Dewey's ideas.
16. Ted came to New York to visit Debbie. "I thought he was the first high school person who was approaching schooling in the same way I was," she said. They had dinner in East Harlem to discuss her starting a high school. "We were throwing around ideas about what a high school could be. I was flying high!" Subsequently she reached out to Steve Phillips, the head of alternative schools in New York City. "He went with me to Albany to see Dr. Thomas Sobol, the state commissioner, who had been principal of an alternative school in Westchester. As soon as I met Tom, it was like we were old friends, he was so enthusiastic. He said, 'I trust you.' He was always there for me. That was true also about Tony and Ted." Debbie said that Linda Darling-Hammond, who was at Columbia University at the time, supported and championed the idea as well. "She was careful and thoughtful," Debbie said. "And we got permission to be exempt from the Regents from Tom" (Debbie Meier, in discussion with the author, January 15, 2023).
17. Michael S. Roth, *Beyond the University: Why Liberal Education Matters* (Yale University Press, 2014), 175.
18. Francis Wayland Parker Papers 1857–1904, Hanna Holborn Gray Special Collections Research Center, University of Chicago Library. In a memorial service delivered at the University of Chicago in 1902, Dewey said that Parker was "noble and single-minded" and that "his belief in the unrealized possibilities of the art of teaching was sublime."
19. Warren Bennis and Patricia Ward Biederman, *Organizing Genius: The Secrets of Creative Collaboration* (Perseus Books,

1997). The excerpts that I selected came from various pages in the book.

20. James W. Stigler and James Hiebert, preface to *The Teaching Gap: Best Ideas from the World's Teachers for Improving Education in the Classroom*, 2nd ed. (Free Press, 2009).
21. But this was not always the case. As Linda Darling-Hammond and Jeannie Oakes wrote in *Preparing Teachers for Deeper Learning*, after the Civil War, teachers in African American schools "used pedagogy that encouraged students to question what they read and to engage in critical thinking" (Harvard Education Press, 2019), 15.
22. Based on a poem by Warsan Shire, the first Young Poet Laureate for London.
23. This was in October 2010, back when our high school was housed inside our very first location: the East Harlem Council for Community Improvement, a community center next to the Wagner housing projects on East 120th Street near the FDR Drive.
24. When we met Carol, she had already written several books, as both an author and a coauthor, including *The Advisory Guide* (with Rachel A. Poliner, Educators for Social Responsibility, 2004) and *Getting Classroom Management RIGHT* (Educators for Social Responsibility, 2009). Since that time, we have studied her new work, *Shifting Gears: Recalibrating Schoolwide Discipline and Student Support* (with Michele Tissiere and Nicole Frazier, Engaging Schools, 2015), a comprehensive guide to school culture and discipline, and her magnum opus, *Engaged Classrooms: The Art and Craft of Reaching and Teaching All Learners* (with Michele Tissiere et al., Engaging Schools, 2019), as core texts at HVA.

25. Carol Lieber, in discussion with the author, July 18, 2022. Sadly, Carol passed away unexpectedly in October of that same year.
26. For example, when she explained how to teach social-emotional skills with a protocol called "Model, Teach, Practice, Assess," she gave us practical tools but also wanted us to know that the concept had originated in the 1970s with the learning theory of social cognitive psychologist Albert Bandura, one of the preeminent psychologists of the twentieth century. Dr. Bandura coined the terms *self-efficacy* and *modeling*. He authored over a dozen books, including the seminal *Social Learning Theory* (1977).
27. The Harkness table was originally introduced in 1929 at Phillips Exeter Academy.
28. Deborah Loewenberg Ball is professor and former dean of the University of Michigan School of Education, founder of Teaching Works, and author of over 150 publications, including "The Work of Teaching and the Challenge for Teacher Education" in *Journal of Teacher Education* 60, no. 5 (2009). Magdalene Lampert is professor emeritus of education at the University of Michigan and author of *Teaching Problems and the Problems of Teaching* (Yale University Press, 2003) and leader of the "Learning Teaching in, from, and for Practice" project for developing teacher education pedagogy at the University of Washington, the University of Michigan, and UCLA.

CHAPTER 4

1. James Baldwin, "The Art of Fiction No. 78," interview by Jordan Elgrably, *Paris Review*, no. 91 (Spring 1984).
2. Bob Dylan, "2016 Nobel Lecture in Literature," recorded June 4, 2017, Los Angeles, CA.

3. HVA charter application.
4. Albert Einstein, quoted in William Miller, "Death of a Genius," *Life*, May 2, 1955, 64.

CHAPTER 5

1. Sam Wineburg, *Why Learn History (When It's Already on Your Phone)* (University of Chicago Press, 2018), 134.
2. Conley coined the term *college readiness*, the idea that certain kinds of academic preparation are essential to do well in college. David T. Conley, *College Knowledge: What It Really Takes for Students to Succeed and What We Can Do to Get Them Ready* (Jossey-Bass, 2005); *Conley Readiness Index* (Pearson, 2017); *A Complete Definition of College and Career Readiness* (Educational Policy Improvement Center, 2012); *College and Career Ready: Helping All Students Succeed Beyond High School* (Jossey-Bass, 2010); "Rethinking College Readiness," *New Directions for Higher Education* 2008, no. 144 (2008): 3–13; and *Mixed Messages: What State High School Tests Communicate About Student Readiness for College* (Center for Educational Policy Research, University of Oregon, 2003).
3. Joan Richardson, "College Knowledge: An Interview with David Conley," *Phi Delta Kappan* 92, no. 1 (September 2010), 29.
4. This is not to say that there is no place for memorization. There is great value in knowing important facts, such as the times tables, the branches of government, and so on, and committing them to memory. In *Horace's School* (65–66), Sizer provides a list of examples of things that students should be able to recite by memory, which he suggests could be part of a final exhibition: "Draw a map of the world, freehand. Draw a map of the United States, freehand, and accurately. Identify and answer questions about the current United States president and vice president, your state's two US senators, etc. Present

a timeline since 1750 that you have assembled over the last several years and be prepared to answer questions about any event that appears on it."

5. Ted Sizer, "Opening Remarks, Fall Forum 2000, Providence, Rhode Island," *Horace* 25, no. 2 (2009).
6. Ann Cook, correspondence with the author, March 21, 2023, and Debbie Meier, in discussion with the author, January 14, 2023. The New York Performance Standards Consortium was based largely on the ideas that Ted championed and was initially mostly comprised of schools from his Coalition of Essential Schools, including Debbie's. Authorization to grant diplomas using performance-based assessment came in the form of a waiver signed by New York State Commissioner Dr. Thomas Sobol in 1995 in response to a request from Debbie and Steve Phillips, the superintendent of New York's alternative schools division. The consortium was formally created in 1998. Students were still required to pass the ELA Regents.
7. More than a decade later, the Regents began a process to consider shifting state policy to incorporate the kinds of quality assessments we had discussed, such as the IB and performance-based assessment.
8. Winnie Hu, "Scarsdale Adjusts to Life Without Advanced Placement Courses," *New York Times*, December 6, 2008. It was the 2007–08 school year when the AP courses were phased out.
9. John Klemme, "Advanced Placement Becomes 'Advanced Topics,'" *Education Week*, September 29, 2008.
10. In the case of Montessori, children in PreK work on academic tasks for two and a half hours each day during what is called "work time." In the case of the IB, students engage in long-term research projects over the course of an entire year.
11. Sizer, "Opening Remarks."

12. International Baccalaureate Organization, *Assessment Principles and Practices: Quality Assessment in a Digital Age* (International Baccalaureate Organization, 2018), 98.

CHAPTER 6

1. Ted Sizer, "On Changing Secondary Schools: A Conversation with Ted Sizer," interview by Ron Brandt, *Educational Leadership* 45, no. 5 (1988), 31. Ted also discussed this idea on many other occasions over the years.
2. This is not to say that there is no place for direct instruction or lecture. There are certainly instances in which this strategy is helpful, so long as it is not the only or dominant strategy.
3. Zaretta Hammond, *Culturally Responsive Teaching and the Brain: Promoting Authentic Engagement and Rigor Among Culturally and Linguistically Diverse Students* (Corwin, 2015), 14.
4. Sonja Brookins Santelises, *Checking In: Do Classroom Assignments Reflect Today's Higher Standards?* (The Education Trust, 2015), 4.
5. Mihaly Csikszentmihalyi, *Flow: The Psychology of Optimal Experience* (HarperPerennial, 1991).
6. John Dewey, *The Child and the Curriculum* (University of Chicago Press, 1902), 33.
7. Edward L. Deci and Richard M. Ryan, *Intrinsic Motivation and Self-Determination in Human Behavior* (Plenum, 1985); R. M. Ryan and E. L. Deci, "Self-Determination Theory and the Facilitation of Intrinsic Motivation, Social Development, and Well-Being," *American Psychologist* 55, no. 1 (2000); and Deci and Ryan, "The 'What' and 'Why' of Goal Pursuits: Human Needs and the Self-Determination of Behavior," *Psychological Inquiry* 11, no. 4 (2000). Several frameworks originated in twentieth-century cognitive and social psychology, including

Self-Determination Theory as well as Self-Regulated Learning Theory (not to be confused with self-regulation of emotions). Zimmerman refers to three components of Self-Regulated Learning: forethought, performance, and self-reflection.

8. Robert P. Moses and Charles E. Cobb Jr., *Radical Equations: Civil Rights from Mississippi to the Algebra Project* (Beacon Press, 2001).
9. Paul Revere Pierce, *The Origin and Development of the Public School Principalship* (University of Chicago Press, 1935), 11.
10. When teaching math, our central principle is problem-based learning, which develops students' conceptual understanding. In addition, a well-known instructional method we use, particularly with students who struggle with math or those who have learning disabilities, is the "CRA" (concrete, pictorial, abstract) sequence. This approach, based on Bruner's theory of cognitive development, was advanced by the Singapore education community, among others, in the early 1980s. In the CRA sequence, students first use physical objects to work on solving math problems (the "concrete" phase). Next, they draw pictures or visual representations of the idea (the "pictorial" phase), which reinforces their understanding (if the proportions are correct, for example) or illuminates their misconceptions (if incorrect). Finally, they use mathematical symbols and numbers (the "abstract" phase). This method is used mostly for teaching place value, fractions, and geometry, and it is sometimes used in algebra. See Leong Yew Hoong et al., "Concrete-Pictorial-Abstract: Surveying Its Origins and Charting Its Future," *Mathematics Educator* 16, no. 1 (2015): 1–19.
11. This idea has come to be known as competency-based education and has been advocated by a number of research organizations and educational leaders. See Tom Vander Ark, "The Case for Competency-Based Education," *Getting Smart*, November 2, 2018. See also Chris Sturgis and Katherine Casey,

Quality Principles for Competency-Based Education (iNACOL CompetencyWorks, 2018).

12. Jerome Bruner, "The Act of Discovery," *Harvard Educational Review* 31 (1961): 21–32.
13. Grant Wiggins, "Transfer as the Point of Education," *Granted, and . . . Thoughts on Education*, Authentic Education, January 11, 2012.
14. Martha Stone Wiske, "What Is Teaching for Understanding?," in *Teaching for Understanding: Linking Research with Practice*, ed. Martha Stone Wiske (Jossey-Bass, 1998), 72. In 1988, a group at Harvard including Howard Gardner, Vito Perrone, Ron Ritchhart, Karen Hammerness, David Perkins, and Martha Stone Wiske collaborated with teachers on a long-term study that resulted in the book.
15. John D. Bransford et al., eds., *How People Learn: Brain, Mind, Experience, and School* (Commission on Behavioral and Social Sciences and Education, National Research Council, National Academy of Sciences, 1999).
16. John H. Flavell, "Metacognitive Aspects of Problem Solving," in *The Nature of Intelligence*, ed. Lauren B. Resnick (Lawrence Erlbaum, 1976), 231–236. See also Flavell, "Metacognition and Cognitive Monitoring: A New Area of Cognitive-Developmental Inquiry," *American Psychologist* 34, no. 10 (1979).
17. John Hattie, "Anticipation-Action-Reflection Cycle," *OECD Learning Compass 2030*, 2020.
18. International Baccalaureate Organization, *Theory of Knowledge Guide*, IB Diploma Programme (International Baccalaureate Organization, 2020), 5–6.
19. David Ropeik, "The L'Aquila Verdict: A Judgment Not Against Science, but Against a Failure of Science Communication," *Scientific American*, October 22, 2012; and Edwin Cartlidge,

"Italy's Supreme Court Clears L'Aquila Earthquake Scientists for Good," *Science*, November 20, 2015. The verdict was overturned on appeal in 2015 by Italy's Supreme Court in Rome.

20. Lauren B. Resnick et al., *Accountable Talk: Instructional Dialogue That Builds the Mind*, Educational Practices Series 29 (UNESCO International Bureau of Education, 2018), 14–15. Note that *accountable talk* is a registered trademark of the University of Pittsburgh.
21. Sarah Michaels et al., *Accountable Talk Sourcebook: For Classroom Conversation That Works* (Institute for Learning, University of Pittsburgh, 2016).
22. Resnick, *Accountable Talk*, 15.
23. Anne Ruggles Gere, *Roots in the Sawdust: Writing to Learn Across the Disciplines* (National Council of Teachers of English, University of Washington, 1985). Ruggles writes, "Writing is uniquely suited to foster abstract thought. As cognitive psychologists and composition theorists have noted, writing is an extremely focused activity which [can] lead to more coherent and sustained thought" (10).
24. Grant Wiggins, "Seven Keys to Effective Feedback," *Educational Leadership* 70, no. 1 (2012), 10–16.
25. John Hattie and Shirley Clarke, *Visible Learning: Feedback* (Routledge, 2019), 5.

CHAPTER 7

1. Agency was also an ever-present part of our discussions with the group. Agency—or, as most of them called it, student independence—was woven into the way they taught, the books they had written, the advice they gave us. They had each come to this stance in a different way: Shelley from examining Montessori, Donna from studying Brian Cambourne's

work at Teachers College, Ron as a student teacher of the veteran teachers who would later go on to found Responsive Classroom.

2. David T. Conley, *Getting Ready for College, Careers, and the Common Core: What Every Educator Needs to Know* (Jossey-Bass, 2014), 73.
3. Martin Haberman, "The Pedagogy of Poverty Versus Good Teaching," *Phi Delta Kappan* 73, no. 4 (1991): 290–294. Haberman wrote that he had observed the pedagogy of poverty since he started teaching in 1958. A later version was published as a Kappan Classic in 2010, along with a follow-up piece in October 2010: "11 Consequences of Failing to Address the Pedagogy of Poverty," *Phi Delta Kappan* 92, no. 2 (2010): 45.
4. Maria Montessori, *From Childhood to Adolescence* (Clio Press, 1948), 65.
5. International Baccalaureate Organization, "Key Elements of an IB Education," *Approaches to Teaching and Learning*, April 14, 2015.
6. Daniel Goleman, *Working with Emotional Intelligence* (Bantam, 1998).
7. Theodore R. Sizer and Nancy Faust Sizer, *The Students Are Watching: Schools and the Moral Contract* (Beacon Press, 1999), 17. Carol called this "group agreements," Ron called it "norms," Ruth Charney called it "collaborative rule-making." We decided to call it "class commitments."
8. Carol Miller Lieber, *Getting Classroom Management RIGHT: Guided Discipline and Personalized Support in Secondary Schools* (Educators for Social Responsibility, 2009), 101–105.
9. Ted Wachtel, *Defining Restorative* (International Institute for Restorative Practices Graduate School, 2016), 3.
10. We originally learned this process from Carol when she was coaching us, and it is now a core part of our discipline

system. Additional information can be found in *Shifting Gears: Recalibrating Schoolwide Discipline and Student Support* by Carol Miller Lieber, Michele Tissiere, and Nicole Frazier (Engaging Schools, 2015).

CHAPTER 8

1. Kurt Hahn, founder of the Gordonstoun school, the Salem school, Outward Bound, and the United World Colleges, was one of the most influential educators of the twentieth century. He also contributed to the framework for the International Baccalaureate. Hahn had once seen the phrase "there is more in you than you think" etched into the stone of a Belgian church, and it became the Gordonstoun school motto.
2. William Deresiewicz, "The Disadvantages of an Elite Education," *American Scholar*, June 1, 2008.
3. Philip W. Jackson, "The Student's World," *Elementary School Journal* 66, no. 7 (1966): 345–357. Jackson coined the term *hidden curriculum*. See also *Life in Classrooms* (Holt, Rinehart and Winston, 1968).
4. Rainer Maria Rilke, *Letters to a Young Poet* (Vintage Books, 1986), 18–19.
5. We had an advisory system from the very beginning at HVA, inspired by Larry, who had advisory at High Tech High, and Dennis, who had incorporated advisory into his schools since the 1970s. We subsequently learned more about it from Carol, who told us that the first advisory system she knew of had been established by F. E. Clerk, principal of New Trier High School in suburban Chicago's North Shore, in 1928.

CONCLUSION

1. Rabbi Menachem Mendel Schneersohn, the Lubavitcher Rebbe, quoting Rabbi Yosef Yitzhak Schneersohn quoting

Rabbi Sholom Dovber Schneersohn, *Igros Kodesh*, 1929, Vol. 16, Letter #5814, 107.

2. Linda Darling-Hammond et al., "What Matters Most: Teaching for America's Future," *Report of the National Commission on Teaching and America's Future*, September 1996, 9–10.
3. Linda Darling-Hammond and Jeannie Oakes, *Preparing Teachers for Deeper Learning* (Harvard Education Press, 2019), 11–13.
4. Vito Perrone, "Opening Remarks, Meeting of North Dakota Study Group," 1998, Dean Vito Perrone Records, University of North Dakota, Elwyn B. Robinson Department of Special Collections, Chester Fritz Library. The group started in November 1972 with seventeen educators from around the country, including Debbie Meier, Eleanor Duckworth, Lillian Weber, Patricia Carini, Joseph Featherstone, Bill Ayers, Ann Cook, and Herb Mack, who gathered in North Dakota for three days to discuss concerns regarding reading assessment. The group continued to discuss key educational issues of the day, meeting for an annual convening every February in various locations, although it was still known as the North Dakota Study Group.
5. Grant Wiggins, "A Minor Rant on a Recent Article on Question-Based Teaching—This Is New?????," *Granted, and . . . Thoughts on Education*, Authentic Education, November 3, 2011.
6. In 1919, the Progressive Education Association was founded in Washington, DC, based on seven principles, including intrinsic motivation, social-emotional learning, rich curriculum, and teacher as facilitator of student thinking. (While deeper learning has its roots in progressive education, it concerns itself with pedagogy, not politics, and is grounded in learning science.)

7. Pedro Noguera, Linda Darling-Hammond, and Diane Friedlander, "Equal Opportunity for Deeper Learning," *Deeper Learning Research Series*, October 2015, 3.
8. Maria Montessori, *The Advanced Montessori Method* (Frederick A. Stokes, 1917), 139. Her ideas about student self-direction were revolutionary at the time.
9. Jerome S. Bruner et al., *A Study of Thinking* (Chapman & Hall, 1956). See also "The Act of Discovery," *Harvard Educational Review* 31 (1961), in which Bruner writes about the teacher as facilitator and the value of intrinsic motivation, and *Beyond the Information Given: Studies in the Psychology of Knowing* (W. W. Norton, 1973).
10. Alec Peterson, *Arts and Science in the Sixth Form* (Oxford Department of Educational Studies, 1960).
11. Comer developed the Comer Process, a system that focuses on social-emotional child development and building close bonds between and among students, staff, and families. It has been utilized in hundreds of schools across the country. Based at the Yale Child Study Center, he has written numerous books, as both an author and a coauthor, including *Rallying the Whole Village: The Comer Process for Reforming Education* (Teachers College Press, 1996).
12. James P. Comer in "Building Schools as Communities: A Conversation with James Comer," by John O'Neil, *Educational Leadership*, Association for Supervision and Curriculum Development, May 1, 1997, Vol. 54, No. 8.
13. Meier's "Habits of Mind" framework, designed in 1985, has been replicated by countless schools across the country and was a precursor to graduate profiles. When asked why she called it *habits* as opposed to *skills*, she said, "I want all this to be automatic for students, part of who they are. I want students to automatically ask certain kinds of questions when they hear

something. They should be curious and respond, 'How do you know, what's the evidence, where does that come from?' When students hear something, I want them to not turn off but turn on" (Debbie Meier, in discussion with the author, January 29, 2023).

14. David Perkins, "What Is Understanding?," in *Teaching for Understanding: Linking Research with Practice*, ed. Martha Stone Wiske (Jossey-Bass, 1998), 40.
15. Linda Darling-Hammond et al., "What Matters Most: Teaching for America's Future," *Report of the National Commission on Teaching & America's Future*, September 1996.
16. Kathleen Cushman, "Ted, Expecting Us," *Horace* 25, no. 2 (2009).
17. In 1984, Ted's Coalition of Essential Schools articulated a set of common principles that guided a generation of educators. These included depth over coverage, personalization, teacher as coach, demonstration of mastery, and more. To cite just one example, Ted was introduced to the concept of exhibitions at Andover, and he codified and popularized it in his 1992 book, *Horace's School*.
18. James Baldwin, "A Talk to Teachers," originally delivered October 16, 1963, subsequently published in *Saturday Review*, December 21, 1963, reprinted in *The Price of the Ticket: Collected Nonfiction: 1948–1985* (Saint Martin's Press, 1985).

ABOUT THE AUTHOR

DR. DEBORAH KENNY is the founder of Harlem Village Academies and the Deeper Learning Institute and is one of the most influential educators in the country. Deborah has been honored with the Columbia University Teachers College Distinguished Alumni Award, has been included on Oprah's Power List and *Esquire*'s Best and Brightest, and is regularly featured in national media. She holds a PhD from Columbia University in comparative international education and a BA from the University of Pennsylvania. She is the mother of three grown children and lives in New York City.